COUNTRY DUPPY & JONKANOO JAMBOREE

ASTON COOKE

authorHOUSE®

AuthorHouse™
1663 Liberty Drive
Bloomington, IN 47403
www.authorhouse.com
Phone: 1-800-839-8640

Published by AuthorHouse   10/17/2014

ISBN: 978-1-4969-4842-7 (sc)
ISBN: 978-1-4969-4841-0 (e)

FOREWORD

When a playwright/dramatist as successful and prolific as Aston Cooke decides to offer his plays for publication, it is a time to rejoice. One can rest assured that theatre-lovers, students, researchers and cultural practitioners have been granted access to even more Jamaican/Caribbean material of substance. Audiences both regionally and internationally have had the opportunity to enjoy Cooke's productions and can attest to the quality of his writing. Having directed two of his plays, I can attest to his attention to detail and the authenticity of his writing style. His genuine love for the Jamaican/Caribbean persona shines through in his realistic portrayals of character, as revealed through dialogue.

With that said it must be noted that Cooke also has a gift for creating exciting dialogue that leaps off the page and makes staging easy. The gift extends into the unerring eye for seeing and presenting 'theatrical moments' laden with that rich and colourful sensibility and aesthetic which is totally Caribbean. In such moments, Cooke word-paints strong opposing characters into delicious contrast with each other. And yet, he doesn't just paint with broad and colourful Caribbean brush strokes. He invests his characters with a sense of 'sweet irony' and 'smooth wit' so they breathe life like living proverbs and metaphors walking easily from page to stage. There is no doubt that his observance of the nuances and subtleties of character is exemplary.

It is not surprising that the first plays to be published are Country Duppy and Jonkanoo Jamboree. One of Cooke's stylistic strengths shines through in his sensitive treatment of rural folk where he takes them and places them in dramatic conflict with their own traditional beliefs. Another stylistic strength is his ability to present humorous situations fraught with dramatic tension as political satire. Cooke's body of work forces the audience/reader to examine their concepts about themselves as Jamaicans and as Caribbean people. He uses humour to poke holes in preconceived notions about society and get people and ask questions of themselves and where they belong on the social grid between urban and rural; Europe and Africa; uptown or downtown; dancehall or dinky mini; demonstration or tea party; Christianity or Obeah.

As a teacher of Jamaican and Caribbean folk and traditional dance, it was particularly pleasing to see how Cooke infused life into the Jamaican masquerade form of Jonkanoo and how he weaved the Jonkanoo characters into a powerful script. In Jonkanoo Jamboree, Cooke creates a new myth based in Jamaican folktales and folk forms. What is particularly exciting is that although it is clear that he has a penchant for using and addressing cultural forms in his plays, he is not heavy-handed in his application of such forms. It is done in a style that complements the form itself.

Aston Cooke has done a masterful job at storytelling with both Country Duppy and Jonkanoo Jamboree. I feel privileged to have been the first person to direct Jonkanoo Jamboree for the stage and be part of that process of bringing to life the wonderful characters in the play. I know that readers of the play will enjoy the Caribbean fantasy-fiction-like quality and appreciate the juxtaposition of the rural life and the urban aesthetic of the dancehall. Both Country Duppy and Jonkanoo Jamboree are great reads and beautiful scripts ready for staging.

Michael Holgate
Philip Sherlock Centre for the Creative Arts
University of the West Indies
Mona, Kingston 7
Jamaica

COUNTRY DUPPY

First performed at the Barn Theatre, Kingston, Jamaica on Wednesday, July 12, 2000 with the following cast:

Beatrice:	Leonie Forbes
Clara:	Tulip Reid
Moses:	Christopher Daley
Bredda Zacky / Goody:	Peter Heslop
Rocky:	Clifton Danvers

Directed by Michael Nicholson

ACT ONE

ACT I, SCENE 1

MISS BEATRICE'S VERANDAH. LATE EVENING. THE SCENE IS SET IN BAMBOO BELLY DISTRICT SOMEWHERE IN RURAL JAMAICA. MISS BEATRICE LIVES IN A BIG PLANTATION STYLED GREAT HOUSE WITH A LARGE VERANDAH. THE INTRICATE LATTICE WORK OF THE VERANDAH IS PAINTED WHITE AND STRECHES AROUND THE FRONT AND SIDES OF THE HOUSE REMINISCENT OF OLD JAMAICA. THE VERANDAH DOUBLES AS A MEETING PLACE AND A WORK AREA FOR MISS BEATRICE WHO IS THE ONLY DRESSMAKER IN THE VILLAGE. AN OLD AND OBSIOUSLY WORKED SINGER SEWING MACHINE ADORNS ONE END OF THE VERANDAH. WHEN THE LIGHTS COME UP, BEATRICE IS TAKING CLARA'S MEASUREMENT FOR A NEW DRESS.

BEATRICE: Stand up straight Clara so me can get di right measurement fah you waist. Make me see, thirty-two, dat no too tight?

CLARA: Thirty-two which part Miss Beatrice? How you get my little wire waist to be thirty-two? Yuh must mean centimetre. Measure it again please ma'am.

BEATRICE: See, me still get thirty-two. Thirty-two and a half inches. How long you want it? Here so?

CLARA: You mad Miss Beatrice mam? After a no maxi frock you a make ma'am? Is a tight mini dress me want. Is dat dem a wear a Kingston now. Dat is di lick. Ah di 'bling-bling'.

3

BEATRICE: Clara, you can't wear mini dress go ah funeral. Duppy will box yuh down.

CLARA: Me nah go ah Mammie funeral Miss Beatrice. I don't venture into those places.

BEATRICE: Look like nobody in di whole ah Bamboo Belly District going to Ol' Mammie funeral at all.

CLARA: Serve her right. Live bad and everybody treat yuh bad even in death.

BEATRICE: So what dem going to do with all of dat whole heap of food; rum, bread, fish and plenty white rum?

CLARA: Me nah go ah di funeral, but me will nyam di wagga-wagga food and drink di free rum.

BEATRICE: So if is not di funeral you deh go, what you want new frock for?

CLARA: Ah Kingston me ah go. Me have a little business looking about in town early next week.

BEATRICE: How you to go ah town and miss all of di funeral excitement inna Bamboo Belly?

CLARA: Dat can't miss me mi Miss B. Me will catch a Kingston before day light Monday morning. Me will come back before di nine night set-up.

BEATRICE: Is what kind of bandooloo business you doing in Kingston why you have to travel at night? Are you a duppy?

CLARA: Ah U.S. embassy me a go mam. Me have an eight o'clock appointment. Me have to go a farrin fah di new year. Me have to get di visa dis year, by di hook or by di crook.

BEATRICE: Dem soon tired fi see you face down a dat place Clara. How you manage get another appointment at the embassy?

CLARA:	New year, new passport, different picture, change of name and occupation. A new identity.
BEATRICE:	You going go on until dem hold on on you one of dese days and send you go a work-house.
CLARA:	Di only work-house me a go is to America so me can make some good US dollar. Me tired a hussle dollars from di tourist dem now man. One little fassy looking tourist man me meet di other day in Ochie say him would a sponsor me fi go to Philadelphia.
BEATRICE:	So why yuh never go on? Well how come you miss out on dat?
CLARA:	A smaddy him did ah look Miss Beatrice. And me never inna dat so me just set him on Shirly. She married him and tek off.
BEATRICE:	Is not everybody cut out fah di farrin business you know.
CLARA:	Miss B, look on me and see if you no see farrin just a bawl out on me? Is she same one, Shirly, dat send dis piece of material for me to make di frock. It nice eeh?
BEATRICE:	It pretty fah true. How you want di frock? What style yuh want it?
CLARA:	Designer mini to fit me little wire-waist 'Lisa-Hanna' body. No laugh after me ma'am. Me must get di visa dis time and lef di whole a unno right here so back ah hog.
BEATRICE:	Back ah hog? Is dat yuh calling Bamboo Belly now? Di bus always turns around. One day you will have to come right back.
CLARA:	Back to what? Dry crackers and river water? Dutty gal and bare-back white rice. Is wha do yuh Miss B, is steak and champagne I want fi nyam and drink. Nutten naah go on right here so.

BEATRICE:	Go into Montego Bay to look fah work. I hear that Sandals Hotel is opening another branch near to the harbour.
CLARA:	Me not doing any slave work inna hotel ma'am. Is hairstyling and cosmetology I did study a Madam Rose Leon School of Beauty Culture in Kingston. I do hair, manicure and pedicure.
BEATRICE:	Which part you tink yuh can get hairdressing work in farrin. Is domestic you going have to do. Or look after old sick people.
CLARA:	After nothing no wrong with domestic Miss Beatrice. If is dat me have to do me will do it. Jamaica domestic work and farrin domestic wuk is not di same thing you know Miss B.
BEATRICE:	Why yuh don't open a little business a Bamboo Belly?
CLARA:	Me no have dat kind of money right now. And bank nah lend money again. Dem a look bail out dem self. So me was a think dat me could a go a farrin go look di money.
BEATRICE:	Well, farrin dollars strong. But in di meantime, I will settle fah Jamaican dollars. I need half of the payment as deposit on this frock.
CLARA:	Larks Miss B, mam. When I come back from Kingston I will set you up fully. Make di frock and I will owe you on it.
BEATRICE:	Nothing no work so Clara. Well, I will owe yuh di frock den.
CLARA:	All right Miss B. Me nah thief yuh mam. See half of di money here. (SHE COUNTS OUT THE CASH AND HANDS IT OVE.) Me can get it Sunday morning?
BEATRICE:	Make sure you pass by Saturday morning and come fit it.

CLARA: Tcho, me no have to fit dat man. I trust you. As long as you don't mek fool-fool Moses put him finger on it.

BEATRICE: Moses not a dressmaker, Clara. Moses wuk a ground and go a riverside go catch janga.

CLARA: Den me no come here come see Moses a sew Miss Beatrice? Me tek me two eyes see him around the machine a sew clothes. Say him a make tie to wear go a church. Den another time me hear him say is barbering him want to do. Who inna dem rightful self would make Moses trim dem head? Look pon him head.....him favour mad smaddy.

BEATRICE: Poor Moses. He really took Mammie's death to heart. He used to look after her place fah her and she gave him food in return.

CLARA: Moses lick him head yuh hear Miss Beatrice. Ever since him mumma dash him away a riverside, him lick him head on rockstone. Him should a lucky for a woman like you to give him a roof over his head.

BEATRICE: I do what I can do fah him. Just like Moses in the bible Clara. He is gone to the churchyard to help dig Mammie's grave. When yuh a pass, call him for me yuh hear? And Miss Clara, please, remember to come fit di frock if yuh want it to look good.

BLACK-OUT

ACT I, SCENE 2

MISS BEATRICE'S VERANDAH. SUNDAY MORNING. CLARA FITS HER
NEW OUTFIT WHILE MISS BEATRICE MAKES ADJUSTMENT TO THE
FROCK WITH PINS. CLARA FIDGETS AS SHE ATTEMPTS TO GET A
GLIMPSE.

BEATRICE: Clara, if yuh don't stop spinning, di pin and needle dem will jook you. Please stay one place and don't move till me tell yuh. How is dat length? Is di waist too tight? Yuh tink it needs a dart in di bust?

CLARA: Den how yuh a fix it and me nah see it Miss Beatrice. Yuh should a have a mirror out here so we look on we self.

BEATRICE: Clara, keep yuh clappers quiet and mek me fix di frock properly nuh. I am sure yuh don't want to favour heng-pon-nail when yuh go a Kingston.

CLARA: Me can't favour dat Miss Beatrice. Everyting you make look better than dem gyal a town. After dem don't look good. Even if dem come with Dolce & Gabana, Mossimo and Versace, me will shock out a town inna my Miss B's original design. (BOTH WOMEN LAUGH OUT LOUD. THERE IS A KNOCK AT THE GATE) Who is dat? Who is dat?

ZACKY: Who is dat? Yuh can't stay inside there and a bawl out a who dat? Open di gate if you want to find out a who dat.

BEATRICE: Well stay out dere den. Clara, can you see who it is? Climb up on di platform and see ah who.

CLARA CLIMBS ON THE RAILING OF THE VERANDAH TO GET A VIEW
THE STREET.

CLARA: Yes. Is Obeah Man Bredda Zacky from Falmouth. Yes, a him fah true. Him dress to puss-back-foot. Did you send to call him?

BEATRICE: Send to call him fah what? A wonder what him could a want?

CLARA: Yuh don't have to call Bredda Zacky. Once somebody dead inna any district in Jamaica, him will find it. He sniffs out dead like a John Crow. (LOUDER TO ZACKY) Yes, sir, can we help you?

ZACKY: (OFF STAGE) I can hear your melodious voice but your picturesque face eludes me.

CLARA: His mouth is sweet like a politician. What yuh want up here? What brings you to Bamboo Belly?

ZACKY: I am looking for di dead yard. I got a call. Is dis where I can find Miss Beatrice?

CLARA: Yes, Miss Beatrice lives here but she is not dead. (WHISPERS TO BEATRICE) Miss B, is you him ah look fah.

BEATRICE: Coming. Clara don't move. Let me go to the gate. Remember di pin dem. (BEATRICE HEADS TO THE GATE TO GREET ZACKY)

BREDDA ZACKY PUSHES OPEN THE GATE AND MAKES HIS WAY THROUGH THE YARD. HE IS A CHARISMATIC AND SOMEWHAT SHIFTY MIDDLE-AGED OBEAH MAN. HE IS HIGHLY RESPECTED BY SOME AND FEARED BY OTHERS. ZACKY IS DRESSED IN AN OLD GREY THREE-PIECE SUIT WITH A RED SHIRT AND A COLOURFUL TIE. HE WEARS HUGE SILVER RINGS ON BOTH HANDS AND CARRIES A PECULIARLY DESIGNED WOODEN STAFF.

ZACKY: I feel di presence of Beelzebub. (HE CIRCLES THE YARD AND MUTTERS A PRAYER) Away Satan. Away Lucifer.

CLARA:	(MOCKING) Preach it Pastor, amen. Is Mammie spirit in here. Away wicked Mammie. Away evil Mammie.
BEATRICE:	Hello. Excuse me sar. What can I do for you sar?
ZACKY:	What a bright and pleasant morning? A morning only interupted by spirits, invaded by an evil one. Good Morning, I am Brother Zachariah Emanuel Tomlinson at your service Sister Beatrice. Reporting fah duty.
BEATRICE:	Reporting where? For which duty? I didn't send to call any obeah man.
ZACKY:	Never. I am not an obeah man. I am a man of God. I am Jamaica's most respected and honoured professional prayer warrior.
CLARA:	Prayer awrrior my head. That's what you call yourself now? Same difference. Miss Beatrice never send to call a soul.
ZACKY:	She didn't request me personally. But I got a message. A message from the higher messenger. So here I am at your service.
CLARA:	Bredda Zacky, yuh nuh hear what di lady say sir? She nuh want no Obeah Man, she nuh want no Prayer Warrior, she nuh want no duppy tier.
ZACKY:	Sister, you know better than to chase away the messenger of the Lord. Both of you need protection. You both need guard.
CLARA:	We have protection. Miss Beatrice has a sharp cutlas here. (SHE PULLS AN OLD MACHETE FROM THE CORNER OF THE VERANDAH AND POINTS IT AT ZACKY)

ZACKY:	Yuh mad sister? Put that down. A cutlas can't protect you from the dead yuh know. The cutlas will only slip through them.
BEATRICE:	It is true Clara. And you know say dat when coolie duppy ready to tek set, nothing gets rid of dem.
ZACKY:	Tell it to her you wise one. So Sister Beatrice, when is di funeral? When is di nine-night?
BEATRICE:	The funeral is set for Sunday evening up at the Baptist Church. I don't need any protection or interferance, Jesus is my protection. Yuh can go on up to the big yard where Mammie use to live, they may have work for you up there.
ZACKY:	Has anybody tied the body as yet? You know if they're planning to tie di duppy?
CLARA:	After we wouldn't know dat one sir. Wait till her family comes, you can ask dem dat.
ZACKY:	(SURPRISED) Family? But, I heard that the old woman never had a soul.
BEATRICE:	Some people say she has one pickney long time now and nobody don't know which part it deh. Some say she send di pickney gone a farrin to him puppa.
CLARA:	And others say she drown di pickney a riverside.
ZACKY:	Boy pickney or girl pickney?
CLARA:	Dat is di secret. Well, di pickney did name Goody and dat name sound like girl pickney name to me.
BEATRICE:	Clara, mind yuh mouth. Is where yoh get all that information about Mammie's pickney from?

11

CLARA:	Is so mouth say Miss Beatrice. Dem can call my name say a me say so, cause ah me name "Say-so".
ZACKY:	Unno can't sit down and wait till the daughter come before unno tie the duppy. It is not in di interest of the daughter a farrin to tie the duppy. Bamboo Belly people must tie it to protect themselves, especially you Miss Beatrice.
BEATRICE:	Me? Everybody in Bamboo Belly know dat me and Mammie never plant gungo in the same row. But the Lord is my protector from all evil spirits. So, Bredda Zacky, see the dead house up there. Di body is up there, that's where you should go perform your rituals.
ZACKY:	All right. If anything, send to call me. I am not hard to find. When you get to Falmouth, ask for the white house, look for the flags, six red flags, two green and one gold, and a cross painted on the gate. A restless duppy is a troublesome duppy. All duppy must tie. (HE EXITS)
CLARA:	(PAUSE) Tie? Which part him get dem stupidness from Miss B? So is what dem do to tie a duppy?
BEATRICE:	Needle. Dem put nuff needle in her shoes. That way, she stays one place. If she tries to walk, the needles will jook out her daylight. (STICKS CLARA WITH A PIN)
CLARA:	(SCREAMS) Ouch, Miss Beatrice, take time, the pin jook me. Yuh must think me is a duppy mam. If Mammie wants to roam Bamboo Belly, after she no idiot. Needles can't stop her. Mammie duppy will float like star-apple on water.

BLACK-OUT

ACT I, SCENE 3

MISS BEATRICE'S YARD. IT IS EARLY SUNDAY AFTERNOON AND MISS BEATRICE'S YARD HELP, MOSES IS SEATED IN A CORNER OF THE YARD SOBBING. HE CLUTCHES TO AN OLD BIBLE. CLARA SKIRTS INTO THE YARD PASSES MOSES AND HEAD STRAIGHT TO THE VERANDAH.

CLARA: Miss B, where yuh is, Miss B? Miss Beatrice, yuh can't afford to miss dis one. Excitement down ah square mam. Moses, where is Miss Beatrice?

MOSES: Miss Beatrice is inside the house Sister Clara. She will be out shortly. If you are here to collect your frock, it's not ready yet. She says that she still have some hemming to complete.

CLARA: Moses, what you know about frock business? Yuh better go on sweep up Miss Beatrice yard and mind yuh own business. You find yuh mumma whey dash yuh away a riverside yet?

MOSES: The Lord giveth and the Lord also taketh. Mammie was a good mother to me while she was in this wicked world.

CLARA: Don't bother quote bible to me. Whose mother? Cleaning her dirty house doesn't make her your relative yuh know Moses.

MOSES: Miss Clara, you must have respect for the dead. Dat same Mammie yuh see there was me rightful mother. When I was born she was washing clothes at the river and forgot me down dere. When she went back for me, the river washed me away to Miss Beatrice's yard.

CLARA: Yes Moses. Yuh really lick yuh head fah true. Is what yuh want? Yuh heard that your name is on di will? Yuh a go get some of di dead lef?

MOSES: Dead lef? I have no interest in material things Miss Clara. Me is not a parasite. Mammie is me mother. (CRYING) Now she dead and gone (LOUDER)

CLARA: I don't care if Mammie is yuh mumma or yuh puppa. Bawl mi love, make di whole a Bamboo Belly district hear you. (LAUGHS) Satan a bawl fah satan.

MOSES: We are all sinners in the sight of the lord. (HIS CRYING GETS EVEN LOUDER) He has forgiven her for all her bad deeds and has furnished an apartment in heaven to accommodate dear Mammie.

CLARA: Yuh hypocrite and scrumuging brute yuh. Moses, were never so holy when Mammie was alive and sick. A pity di duppy don't fly out a di coffin a cloth yuh a box when you go a di grave side.

MOSES: Don't be unkind. Sister Clara. Let us all in Bamboo Belly be in mourning until Mammie is buried.

CLARA: Speak fah yuh self Moses, all I am here for is the rum and food that's going to be here later. So, when yuh go to the graveside, shove two flasks of whites in yuh pocket and bring for me.

MOSES: How you expect me to think of stealing at a mournful time like dis Miss Clara?

CLARA: Same way how yuh doing it now. You can't fool me Moses. Everybody is coming to the funeral to collect the freeness, you included.

MOSES: Don't involve me in your scam Sister Clara. I could never steal from mi own mother. May her soul rest in peace and be delivered to di almighty.

CLARA:	That duppy will never rest peacefully fah all di wickedness she caused on Massa God's earth. Only Satan can tie down her duppy.
MOSES:	It will be a Christian funeral Sister Clara. And furthermore, no work of Beelzebub is stronger than that of Jehovah. Praise di Lord.
CLARA:	So why did Mammie leave strict instructions to bury her with her big ugly obeah guard ring, the one with the precious ruby stone? They say it is to protect her through her journey.
MOSES:	Nothing like that at all. Guard ring is for the devil, obeah, witch-craft and superstition. Mammie was a Christian, a believer in the Lord Jesus Saviour.
CLARA:	She was the biggest obeah woman in Jamaica. Wickedness was painted on her forehead. I want to get my hand on that guard ring. I would melt it to make gold chain and bracelets and take to the Arcade for sale.
MOSES:	Maybe Mammie left something fah you in her will. Make sure you are present for the reading of the will next week.
CLARA:	No bother sorry fah me Moses. Me no want none of Mammie's ol' bruk that she dead and left. Dat worse than bad obeah.
MOSES:	Well, I had a dream, I got a vision from di Lord that Mammie left me a piece of di land dat stretch's from di church yard all di way back to teacher property.
CLARA:	You never see smoke without fire. So dat is why yuh dress up so? From I came to live in dis district, I have never seen yuh dress like that to do yard work.

MOSES:	I attire myself appropriately to pay my last respect to di deceased. So yuh not going to the churchyard too Sister Clara?
CLARA:	Let the dead bury the dead.

BEATRICE ENTERS WITH A BUNDLE OF UNFINISHED SEWING. SHE PREPARES AN AREA IN A CORNER OF THE VERANDAH, SITS AT THE MACHINE AND STARTS HER SEWING.

BEATRICE:	Quite so. And Moses, I do not want any funeral crosses on me verandah.
CLARA:	Howdy do Miss B? How come yuh a miss di funeral?
BEATRICE:	Mi hearty Clara. I never plan to go to Ol' Mammie funeral. Moses, Yuh tie out di goat dem as yet? When yuh done, please climb di tree and pick two breadfruit fah me, I want to roast dem in the morning for brakfast.
MOSES:	Miss Beatrice, can I get the rest of the evening off so I can attend the funeral of my dearly departed mother?
BEATRICE:	Mother? For all dese years yuh a search fah yuh mother, so yuh find her now? See yah, don't mek me laugh. Christmas gone when yuh collect money from the MP, yuh never have mother nor father, now all of a sudden yuh want time off to "attend the funeral of your mother".
CLARA:	He said he got vision that Mammie put his name him inna her will.
MOSES:	Miss Beatrice, I could never live with me conscience if I miss the funeral, if I am not there to pay my last respect to Mammie yuh know mam.
BEATRICE:	All right Moses, take the time off and go on go pay your last respect to Mammie. Ah hope yuh get what yuh looking for up a graveyard.

MOSES: What me ah look fah mam? Me only hope dat Mammie get a good turn out.

BEATRICE: Happy riddance to you and Mammie. Clear me verandah with di funeral chat. Carry it up a churchyard, dats where it belongs. With you and Pastor Thompson.

CLARA: Dem say dat Pastor Thompson a lick him finger and a fight fah di dead-lef.

BEATRICE: Hurry up and gwan Moses, ah don't want yuh to miss a thing. You and the thieving Pastor can fight and roll down the hillside fah Mammie ol' bruk.

MOSES: Me is not a fighter Miss Beatrice. That is not necessary as me is di only relative dat Mammie has in Bamboo Belly and the rightful inheritor of whatever legacy dat she left behind. (EXITS)

VILLAGERS ARE HEARD SINGING TRADITIONAL CHRISTIAN FUNERAL SONGS. A HILL-SIDE FUNERAL IS IN PROGRESS AND MAY BE SEEN FROM A STRATEGIC POSITION ON MISS BEATRICE'S VERANDAH. CLARA PROPS HERSELF UP AND WATCHES THE PROCEEDINGS AS THE OFFSTAGE SINGING AND SOBBING INCREASE.

CLARA: (LOOKING OUT) Quick Miss Beatrice, di funeral a pass by. Jeezam peas Miss B, look on Bamboo Belly long-gut people dem a bawl and tear out dem morning fah Mammie. All because of little dead-lef. All tough foot Precious and cuff-teeth Dolores. A wha dat she say she wear gone to funeral? From me born, me never see sketel go a funeral. Lord God, Miss Beatrice, Miss Beatrice. (LAUGHS OUT)

BEATRICE: What is it Clara? Mind yuh slip off a di verandah ledge.

CLARA: (STILL LAUGHING AND WATCHING THE FUNERAL) Di funeral sweet Miss Beatrice. Mass Claudie him make a puppalick drop and roll down di hillside. It seems say him is di chief mourner. Teacher deh a di front to.....but stop. Something wrong.....di coffin not moving at all, favour say dem tired. What a waste of good rum doah eeh? Look how Pastor Thompson a sprinkle a whole imperial quart bottle of good Appleton white rum on di coffin.

BEATRICE: Let them all go on weeping and moaning over ol' Mammie. She needs all di prayer dat she can get to carry her through pergutory. The mountains of wickedness and destruction dat she caused when she was alive is worst than Hurricane Charlie, Hurricane Flora and Hurricane Gilbert all put together.

BLACK-OUT

ACT I, SCENE 4

NO CHANGE IN SETTING. GOODY ENTERS THE YARD AND GREETS MISS BEATRICE AND CLARA WHO ARE STILL WATCHING THE FUNERAL PROCEEDINGS IN THE VILLAGE.

GOODY: (OFF STAGE) Haloooooo, Haloooooo, (ENTERS) Haloooooo.

BEATRICE: Haloooooo to you too mam. Clara, is wha kind a jonkano dis eeh ? Can we help you?

GOODY: (FAKE AMERICAN ACCENT) Am I in the right village? What town is this?

BEATRICE: It all depends on which one yuh looking for mam.

GOODY: (ZACKY IS COMICALLY DRESSED AS GOODY. HE ENTERS AND MOVES TO THE VERANDAH) Is this the abodement of Mrs. Mammie McIntosh?

CLARA: What is this? Is what kind of poppy show dis doah eeh? How comes yuh sound like man so? Yuh is man, woman or beast?

BEATRICE: Stop it Clara. Be kind to strangers.

CLARA: She really strange fah true. What a stress?

BEATRICE: (CLEARS THROAT) Beg pardon mam, if it is Miss Mammie abodement yuh looking for, she not "aboding" here anymore.

GOODY: Where she is gone? Is she traveling out of town?

BEATRICE: She is traveling far beyond my dear. If yuh run fast yuh may catch her before she goes down. What is it you want with Mammie?

GOODY: Oh, my apology, let me introduce myself. The name is Goody McIntosh. I am Mammie's daughter.

CLARA:	Daughter? But you don't look like Mammie? Let's see your face. Why is yuh face covered up with the scarf?
GOODY:	You see, I have a case of 'photo-mi-litis'. That means that I have an allergic reaction to the photo sensitive rays of di sunlight. I can't take di hot heat you see.
CLARA:	Yuh ah bleach? Yuh can't tek di sun?
BEATRICE:	Yuh is Mammie pickney from farrin? Welcome to you my dear. That means dat you and Moses is bredda and sista, cause him say dat he is Mammie pickney too.
GOODY:	Moses? I am not aware of any relation by that name. Man, woman, bway or gyal. I got a telegraph cablegram that my mother Mammie was ill so I catch di first flight out of farrin to come and look fah her. Is she seriously ill?
BEATRICE:	Come my love. So you come to look fah Mammie? Take a seat.
CLARA:	No Miss Beatrice, mind she tek her tractor mampie self and bruck down yuh chair mam. (TO GOODY) If you come to see Mammie, then yuh late. Mammie kick di bucket. Yuh just in time fah di burial.
GOODY:	What are yuh talking about lady? Say she kick what mam? Did she injure her big toe in the process?
CLARA:	Dead, she dead. Yuh mumma Mammie is dead.
GOODY:	Lord a feel weak. (SHE STARTS TO CRY) Mammie is deceased?
BEATRICE:	Quick Clara, bring a glass of water fah the nice lady. (CLARA RUSHES INSIDE) Take it easy mam, don't make it get the better of you.

GOODY: (SOBBING) Poor mother Mammie, she has been elevated to her devine saviour and I wasn't here to see her on her journey.

CLARA: (RETURNING WITH A GLASS OF WATER) See the water here nice foreign lady. If yuh rush up there, they will open up di box and mek yuh take a last look pon her.

GOODY: (TAKES GLASS) I only hope I am in time to retrieve my entitlement from the bereavement on the day that the will is explicated.

CLARA: A dead-lef yuh come fah? Yuh couldn't wait till di body cold? Well yuh going have to fight with Moses who claims to be the original pickney plus all ah Bamboo Belly parasites.

GOODY: That's quite alright. I have my birth clarification which will certificate my legal relation.

CLARA: (LOOKING OUT ON THE FUNERAL) You have to move fast if yuh want to catch her. Dem a put the box in the hole now. Wait there, hell a pop. (NOISE OFFSTAGE) Heavens devine Miss Beatrice, they dropped di box. Pure confusion up there. People scattering like ants.

BEATRICE: Clara, yuh making up stories? What is going on up dere?

CLARA: From what I can make out, it looks like a fight or something in the church yard. Everybody grabbing thier shoes, some jumping the fence, some people reach all de way down to the river. I can see Delores again, she just skate the fence over Mass Alex's yard.

GOODY: What is it? Is it a fight or is it local gunmen robbing the mourners? I was warned about the crime down here in Jamaica.

| BEATRICE: | Warned about what? Nowhere in the world have more criminal and thief than America, so no bother with it. |
| CLARA: | Is nothing like dat Miss Goody. Moses a come. Yuh bredda a run come. No track star can beat him. Run Moses run, run till yuh tumble down. |

MOSES DARTS INTO THE YARD. HE CARRIES HIS SHOES AND BIBLE UNDER HIS ARMS. HE IS OUT OF BREATH. HE GOES INSIDE AND RETURNS WITH A CONTAINER OF SALT WHICH HE SPRINKLES AT THE FOUR CORNERS OF THE VERANDAH. HE IS HYSTERICAL AND SPEAKS IN TONGUES.

BEATRICE:	Moses, calm yourself, stand up one place and talk to me. What happened at the burial ground?
MOSES:	Autoclaps at the graveside Miss Beatrice. Alelujah, the Lord is speaking to his people. Amen.
BEATRICE:	Stop the sermon and give us the story. What happened in the churchyard?
MOSES:	First Mammie refused to go up di hill. She put down one piece of dead weight on dem yuh see. Nobody couldn't manage the coffin up di hill. They had to use Missa Rocky cow, Sally, to drag it up di banking of the riverside.
CLARA:	You know what that means Miss B, it meas that somebody alive is responsible for killing Mammie.
BEATRICE:	Clara, stop the accusation, nothing like that.

MOSES: So Miss Beatrice, we finally got the coffin up the hill and just as we were ready to drop it, Sister Adasa suggested that Pastor drenched it with little rum. That was to calm the spirit. Well, when he was sprinkling the rum, we noticed that something inside of the coffin was moving. Everybody thought that the spirit was calm now, but all of a sudden, the coffin broke open and we felt a cool-breeze blow on us, and that was it. The duppy flew out.

BEATRICE: Mammie duppy got away?

MOSES: It was like a cloud. Some white smoke formed a picture of Mammie's face. She went by fast and disappear behind the grave yard and the big cotton tree. Me never know say Mammie could a run so fast.

CLARA: Moses, shut yuh mouth. Yuh too story, nothing can't go like that. You are all wicked so Massa God is talking to unno.

BEATRICE TAKES THE SALT FROM MOSES AND SPRINKLES AT THE FOUR CORNERS OF THE VERANDAH. CLARA FOLLOWS BEHIND HER ECHOING HER EVERY WORD.

BEATRICE: No duppy is coming in this yard tonight, no duppy is taking set tonight. Away evil spirits, crosses and destruction. Away wickedness and tribulation.

BLACK-OUT

ACT I, SCENE 5

MISS BEATRICE'S YARD. IT IS PAST MIDNIGHT AND THE ABORTED BURIAL IS HOURS BEHIND. THE LIGHTING IS EERIE AND THE NIGHT IS PUNCTUATED WITH SOME NATURAL AND SUPERNATURAL SOUNDS. BEATRICE, CLARA AND MOSES RUSH OUT OF THE HOUSE FRIGHTENED.

BEATRICE:	Quick, run outside in the yard. Mind rockstone lick unno. Jeezam peas, Clara, you see how the furniture dem was a shake up themself. The divan and the dresser move from one corner of the room to the other.
CLARA:	Which furniture moved Miss Beatrice? Me never see a thing mam.
MOSES:	My saviour devine. Me can't believe me eye. One big rock stone fly through di window and di pane ah glass never broke. Me see it with me own eye.
BEATRICE:	Sign of the devil Moses. Dog nyam yuh supper if one a dem stone ever hit you. It would make you crippled fah life.
MOSES:	Look deh Miss B, Look deh. (POINTS TO THE YARD)
BEATRICE:	What Moses, what? What is it?
MOSES:	Me head a swell. Look on di duppy, see Mammie deh.
BEATRICE:	Where is she? Where is di duppy Moses? Where is it?

MOSES: It disappeared. Me see two big bright eye in the bush over there near to di lignum vitae tree. They stand up still and stared on me so. So I stare back on him. When the moonlight strike him, all me see was a big red rolling calf with smoke coming out of his nose. Then he vanished. Listen again mam. You hear that? Bell a ring. Duppy.

CLARA: Rolling calf. STANDING FIRM. Come, come inside yah so make I buck yuh.

MOSES: It is running away. It's gone off into the night. It has disappeared.

CLARA: Duppy is afraid of me. Me run duppy, duppy no run me. (SHE SNEAKS UP AND FRIGHTENS MOSES FROM BEHIND) Duppy! Maybe we should go back inside the house, Miss Beatrice.

BEATRICE: Not a soul going back inside that house Clara. That's what the duppy wants us to do so she can throw stones to hit is on the inside.

CLARA: Shame on you Miss B. Don't tell me that you seriously believe in those duppy stories too. All along, I thought that you didn't believe it.

BEATRICE: Clara, the signs are clear. You were inside and heard all the stones on the roof top. You saw with your own eyes when the needle and thread flew out of the machine drawer and nobody touched them. That is the sign of a restless spirit.

CLARA: Restless spirit me rahtid? Miss B, nothing like that. If there was anything like duppy in this country, I would be rich. Because my dead pappa would appear to me in a dream with a million dollar lottery number long time.

BEATRICE: I'm talking bout evilness; your father was a good man. He wouldn't harm a soul.

MOSES:	Him a come back Miss B. See him deh. Di duppy a come back. Di bright light a come. (POINTING BEYOND THE FRONT GATE) Him gone from two bright lights and now it is one.
BEATRICE:	Quiet Moses, make me see for myself. My savior divine it's getting closer. Quick Moses, giveme the two nutmegs, take one and suck on it. See it a come.
CLARA:	Me no see nutten.
MOSES:	Go wash yuh face with rice water and look out there again.
CLARA:	Which part it deh? (SHE LOOKS) Moses and Beatrice di two a unno mussi have matter inna unno eye. Look good and see. It's Rocky from up Florence Hill. (SHE LAUGHS OUT)
BEATRICE:	You right Clara. And favour smaddy trouble him too. (ROCKY ENTERS FROM THE DARK WITH FLASHLIGHT IN HAND) Rocky, what yuh doing out a bush you one at this time of night? Yuh know say yuh nearly frighten we?
ROCKY:	Sorry to a frighten yuh inna di middle a di night so Miss Beatrice. But something vex me mam. Me ah walk up and down from evening, from top-side di church, down a river and back.
CLARA:	We glad to see you Missa Rocky. You come to rescue us or what? Everybody's afraid of duppy. What's happening Missa Rocky?
ROCKY:	(ANGRILY STORMS INTO THE YARD) Anybody sees my cow Sally? All night me deh a ground a look fah di blasted cow and not a sign. From she drop Mammie coffin and tek off inna di bush, I don't set eye on her. Looks like she is lost or just gone roaming Bamboo Belly. I only hope the pickney don't lick her with stone.

BEATRICE:	Moses yuh sure it wasn't Sally you saw earlier?
MOSES:	Miss B, me know rolling calf when me see one. Dat wasn't a cow mam, dat was a bitch-hell-evva duppy cow.
ROCKY:	Sally turned duppy? Unno don't bother confuse me. Moses stop yuh blasted fool-foolishness and answer me. You see Sally or not?
BEATRICE:	Take it easy with Moses yuh hear Rocky. Things have been happening all night since Mammie's funeral. All kinds of mysterious things taking place dat never happened before.
ROCKY:	I don't check fah those things. And furthermore, me no do Mammie anything, she don't have any reason to fool round me and Sally.
CLARA:	Dis getting from bad to worse. Unno see like how I don't want to be involved inna unno crosses, I gone.
BEATRICE:	Clara, don't go out there you one. Where are you going?
CLARA:	Up di hill to me yard Miss B. Where is me frock? Give me, cause I have business ah town to look bout. Ivan mini-van not missing me in di morning, duppy or no duppy.
BEATRICE:	So a little visa to go a farrin is more important dan you life Clara?
CLARA:	Little visa mam? You don't know how important dat one stamp inna you passport is. With dat I can travel and get nuff farrin things. I leave di duppy to cloth Moses, is him relation, so him say.
MOSESL	My mother would never cloth...ah mean harm me.
BEATRICE:	Your mother no? Is same ting Goody a say too. Di two a unno will have to fight over di inheritance.

MOSES:	I'm not fighting a soul mam. I don't tink dat Mammie really and truly did have any other relation.
CLARA:	Think again Moses. You no hear say Mammie tough daughter come from farrin? She is yuh sister. Her name is Goody.
MOSES:	Mammie never ever discuss any other relative with me before she passed away.
CLARA:	Unno going have to roll and fight over her little pittance.
MOSES:	I'm into no fight. Soon di truth will be revealed.
CLARA:	A so me say too. Di duppy will box down whoever a tell di lie.
MOSES:	I am protected in di bosom of di Lord. Plus me have Mammie guard ring. (TAKES RING FROM POCKET)
BEATRICE:	(STARTLED) Yuh have what? What you doing with Mammie guard ring?
MOSES:	Well I decide dat it would be of greater use to me dan to Mammie in di coffin. So me slip it off while I was alone with her in prayer.
BEATRICE:	You mean yuh tief from di dead Moses?
CLARA:	And look how me beg yuh to scuffle one flask a rum bring come and yuh a go on like a prison me a send yuh.
MOSES:	Mammie wouldn't be upset if I am protected. I am her flesh and blood.
BEATRICE:	So is di ring Mammie duppy come back fah. My Saviour pilot me. Moses, tek it off and dash it a dutty.
MOSES:	You crazy Miss B? I can't do without it. Dat would only put me further in di bosom of evilness.

CLARA: Di whole a unno deserve one another. Yuh know what, see unno a morning.

BEATRICE: Clara, don't go out dere.

CLARA: Not a ting up dere Miss Beatrice. Me no fraid mam. And furthermore Rocky will protect me. Rocky, yuh see any duppy out dere sar?

ROCKY: If him out there, I walked over him or favour him fraid fah me.

CLARA: Miss Beatrice, it is quite clear to me dat me is not Ol' Mammie target. She know who she seeking out.

BEATRICE: Alright Clara, I can't force you. But ah tell you what, on you way to town, leave a message a Falmouth fah Bredda Zacky fah me.

CLARA: Miss B, is me you a send go a obeah man? Suppose people see me? I tink yuh never want nutten to do with him mam.

BEATRICE: Clara, right now I willing to take all the help I can get from whomever I can get it from. So if it is from Bredda Zacky, I will take the chance.

CLARA: All right then ma'mm. Write it down, I will tell Ivan to stop in Falmouth when me a go town. Imagine, me Clara Mitchell ah go to obeah man yard at four o clock in di morning...and an no man me ah go tie.

BEATRICE: You know how to find his place?

CLARA: I wouldn't know dat Miss Beatrice, after me never go dere yet.

BEATRICE: Remember di directions him give........When you get to Falmouth, ask for the white house, look for the flags, six red flags, two green and one gold, and a cross painted on the gate

CLARA: Mi only a do it out ah respect fah you Miss Beatrice.

BEATRICE: Thanks Clara. Remember now, don't leave any message. Make sure you talk to him personally and tell him what tek place inna Bamboo Belly district overnight. Tell him to drop everything and come quick-quick.

CLARA: (MOCKINGLY) White house, look fah the flags, six red flags, two green and one gold, and a cross painted on the gate. Me will do it fah you Miss B, me will bring back di duppy conqueror, me will bring back Bredda Zacky, di Prayer Warrior and duppy tier.

                                                    BLACK-OUT

ACT I, SCENE 6

BEATRICE'S YARD. LATE MONDAY EVENING. MOSES IS SITTING IN A
CORNER SORTING GROUND PROVISIONS FROM THE FARM. THERE
IS A COMOTION OUTSIDE AND A KNOCK AT THE GATE. IT IS CLATA
AND ZACKY.

CLARA:	Yuh don't have to knock Bredda Zacky. Me tell yuh say is me run things up here so. Miss Beatrice, Miss Beatrice. Whey she deh?
MOSES:	(TO ZACKY) In the spirit of di Lord I rebuke you. Get behind thee Satan.
CLARA:	Shut yuh mouth Moses. You get behind di house. Come dis way yuh hear Bredda Zacky. Pay no mind to iniquity. Miss Beatrice. CALLING. Miss Beatrice. Whey she deh Moses?
MOSES:	Miss Beatrice will have nothing to do with evil worshipers. What dis man doing in di yard Miss Clara? Why yuh go out of yuh way to bring dis sorcerer into Miss Beatrice decent house?
BEATRICE:	Clara, oh it is you. How yuh come back so quick? Yuh find Bredda Zacky?
CLARA:	Yes ma'am, and see I bring him personally. I stopped there early this morning so me tell him I would come with him when I was returning from town, because you said that I wasn't to return without him.
ZACKY:	You know Sister Beatrice, I know that from my eyes caught the glimpse of your beautiful face, I knew that we would meet again.
BEATRICE:	No bother with yuh sweet talk now Bredda Zacky. And furthermore I am not yuh sister.

ZACKY:	What can I do for you mam. You name the task and it will be done. Bredda Zacky never runs from challenge yet.
BEATRICE:	Yuh remember Ol' Mammie, who died last week?
ZACKY:	How could I forget her? Di same one what never get tied. May her soul rest in peace and may her journey to her saviour be brisk.
BEATRICE:	Well dat is exactly what a call yuh fah, de woman refuse to leave. She isn't ready to go on no journey at all. And to make things worse, she tek set on dis house.
ZACKY:	So yuh want me to get her out? No problem mam, all a have to do is to assist her on di journey, give her a helping hand.
CLARA:	Plus you going have to figure out which one a di pickney dem is Mammie pickney. Two different smaddy ah claim di dead lef.
ZACKY:	What did Mammie dead lef? Did she have money, land or house?
CLARA:	Nuff-nuff gold and silver trinkets. Moses thief one a di ring dem already, see it deh on him finger.
ZACKY:	(HE EXAMINES THE RING ON MOSES' FINGER) Allelujah. Dis is it. See it here.
BEATRICE:	What yuh talking bout Brother Zacky? What is it? What is wrong with Mammie's old guard ring?
ZACKY:	It is anointed with many protective healing oils, she can't travel without it.
CLARA:	Ah tell unno dat long time. So what, it has to go back sar?
ZACKY:	Quite so. It must go back on her finger on or before the nine night or the spirit will never leave Bamboo Belly district.

32

MOSES: (REMOVES RING) See it here sar. Me no bother want it den.

ZACKY: No you have to keep it. Don't make it get out of your hand. Where is the will? Did Mammie leave a will?

MOSES: (HESITANTLY) Yes. She…well…I have di envelope with all di papers that she left which is to be opened and read at the nine night.

ZACKY: Give me everything that you have Moses. (MOSES DIGS DEEP INTO HIS POCKET FOR THE DOCUMENTS AND HANDS THEM TO ZACKY) I will handle everything. Leave it to Bredda Zacky, I will fix it.

BLACK-OUT

ACT I, SCENE 7

MIDDAY MONDAY. MOSES AND ZACKY (GOODY) ARE ON BEATRICE'S VERANDAH.

MOSES:	How comes we never heard Mammie talk about you when she was alive. All of a sudden you turn up. Fah what, to claim di dead lef? I gave over di papers to Bredda Zacky. Furthermore, she never dead lef nothing, so yuh can gallang back a farrin.
GOODY:	Country bway, don't be 'uncourtesy' with me. Do I look like a parasite? And look on you too. My mother couldn't grow a pickney like ah you. Bout yuh is Mammie pickney? Untruth.
MOSES:	Like a vulture on di dead. It is no wonder that di poor lady can't rest in peace. Sake of you, Bamboo Bell is haunted.
GOODY:	Sake a me? Sake a me? Its you who tief di guard ring from my mother. Its you who Mammie is looking fah. She wants her guard ring.
MOSES:	Me no thief no ring. Is take me take it, to protect me from evil like you.
GOODY:	I don't believe in these rural ethnic traditions of witchcraft.
BEATRICE:	(ENTERS FROM THE HOUSE) So unno don't have duppy in farrin Miss Goody?
GOODY:	No doopie at all is in New York. You see, we live in tall buildings and dem can't take elevators. Furthermore, doopies can't live in snow.
BEATRICE:	Ol' Mammie's duppy will climb any mountain and swim any ocean. Spring, summer, autumn or winter.

GOODY:	All of dis tire me out. A feel weak yuh see. Can I get a kotch inside on your bed ma'am?
BEATRICE:	Kotch where yuh want Miss Goody. So where down here you staying? Who you staying with till di will read?
GOODY:	I have a reservation in one of the nice and luxurious super all-inclusive hotels.
BEATRICE:	As bad as yuh mumma was, and still is, me couldn't make yuh come inna we district and go stay a hotel Goody. Not di best, but yuh can kotch up here till after di nine night.
MOSES:	Stay where? Nowhere up here fah her to stay. If she wants to leave right away she can do so. Furthermore since her name is not on di will, she better go back a farrin right now.
BEATRICE:	Moses, you cannot abuse the strange farrin lady like dat. You just met her, what do you know about her?
MOSES:	Dat is di point. These are the sort of people dat di Lord warned us to be weary of. Visitors of di night.
BEATRICE:	Judge not, lest ye be judged Moses.
MOSES:	After nobody not carrying secret fah me mam. Its not only Bredda Zacky we want round here. Send fah di D.C. at the Police station and let him arrest dis fraud woman.
GOODY:	Dats a good idea, sent for di police. I fraid of no one.
BEATRICE:	Unno stop di argument. For as far as I am concerned, you both must be related. You look alike.

MOSES:	Miss Beatrice, don't make a rude to you yah man. Look like who? Look on her face how it tough like tyre.
GOODY:	Liberty comes through carelessness. When you lay with dog, you rise with flea.
MOSES:	Miss Beatrice, you see who di woman wrenk mam. She ah style me as dog now. But I will not respond. I will pray fah you. I will lift you up before di Lord for his forgiveness.
BEATRICE:	All right Moses. Dat is di best thing to do.
GOODY:	Miss Beatrice. I have to go now yuh hear ma'am. I have some business to look after. One more ting mam. Is dere any employment agency in dis district? I need to employ an assistant.
BEATRICE:	Assistant for what Goody?
GOODY:	You know dat when I get all dat inheritance, I may need some assistance to count it out and help me lift it up go a farrin. Ah just joking mam. Di truth is dat I was tinking of renting a car so I may need a driver.
BEATRICE:	You can ask Rocky. He used to drive minibus.
MOSES:	Driver, Rocky drives cow, he is the right man for her to hire.
BEATRICE:	Well, you can find him inna di cow pasture right now with him cow Sally.
GOODY:	All right den, I gotta go. See you at di nine nite Miss Beatrice. See you at di reading of di will Missa Moses. (EXITS)
BEATRICE:	A wha dat?

BLACK-OUT

ACT I, SCENE 8

SAME SETTING AS BEFORE. LATE AFTERNOON. ZACKY IS MEASURING THE AREA IN THE YARD FOR THE NINE NIGHT.

ZACKY:	We should set the upliftment table over here, and di dinki mini drummers can set up on di verandah. This is neutral ground, and furthermore it is the biggest yard in the district. The perfect place fah Mammie nine night.
BEATRICE:	Which nine night? No set-up will be taking place here. Not inna my yard. Dat will only draw her duppy closer.
ZACKY:	Tcho Sister Beatrice man, that is the best way to trap di spirit.
BEATRICE:	She's wont be trapped on my property. Furthermore, Mammie had her own yard. Carry the nine night up there and leave my place alone. That is the dead yard, let Mammie duppy stay up dere.
CLARA:	From what I see, it looks like the duppy is here already. Don't bother spoil up things. Make Moses bring di rum come here man.
BEATRICE:	I don't want any nine night, watchnight or set-up on my property.
CLARA:	Miss Beatrice, think of all di liquor yuh could sell in di yard during di nine night. Me would set up di bar right yasso with di counter deh so with a big drum of Red Stripe beer on ice.
BEATRICE:	Clara, this is not a rum shop, I don't run a bar.

CLARA: Well me will cook a pot a curry goat and try make some money off Mammie. Me will do it if you don't want to do it. Me ah parasite. Me can sell Mammie-drinks, Mammie-chicken, Mammie-Soup and such delight.

MOSES: Don't you dare call Mammie name in those worldian settings.

CLARA: I don't care, she can't touch. I am more worldian than she. I dare her duppy to blow pass me tonight.

BEATRICE: Careful Clara, member say the duppy still on di loose.

ZACKY: We will have to capture it tonight, tonight. Right after di nine night set-up tonight, we will put together a group and go to the graveside.

BEATRICE: Graveside? To do what sir? Go in her mouth? Is dat time she would plaster we.

ZACKY: Not to worry Miss Beatrice, I will plant eleven red peas in the dirt on top of her grave as soon as we are done and that will keep her quiet.

BEATRICE: If that is how we going to hold her tonight well we can't tarry then. All right Bredda Zacky. Keep di set-up round here. But on one condition, me no want Bamboo Belly people dem a walk up and down inside me house looking fah duppy. Cause it is not in there.

ZACKY: Di search fah di spirit is after di set-up Miss Beatrice. Dat is when we get di bravest people dem and head up to di churchyard.

BEATRICE: OK, Clara, gwan up to Brandon Hill and call Mass Rocky and di man dem. Tell dem whats going on down here. Tell dem to gather round here before sun set. Moses, you tell di people dem in the square say di wake is going to be over here tonight, help them bring up all di food dem.

CLARA: Make sure di rum is included. No bother come back here without di rum or you going to get hotter buck than a rolling calf buck tonight. Yuh hear?

BEATRICE: Clara, hurry up and no bother trouble Moses tonight. I will go clear off di verandah and sweep up di yard. Brother Zacky, I hope this will work.

ZACKY: Trust me ma'am, trust me. Twenty years me ah do dis kind ah mission and a duppy never pop me yet.

THE LADIES EXIT IN A HURRY LEAVING ZACKY ALONE IN THE YARD.

ZACKY: (LOOKS AROUND) I catch dem. Dis is easy than I expected. They are all fraid of duppy, perfect target. I'm going to make them fenneh in here tonight at di nine night. All me have to do is fix things so that di coward dem just let off some a di whole heap of money what dem a save up all dis while. The will... where is it? Ah see it Mammie really dead lef. (HE PULLS OPEN THE ENVELOPE AND READS TO HIMSELF) Karamba! Everything is left in Moses' name. Looks like Moses got every pittance left. House for Moses, land for Moses, boot and clothes and bag and pan for Moses. So Moses is the one to samfie? Wait, something isnt right, this will is tampered with to rahtid. Jeezam peas, smaddy rub out all di name and put in 'Moses' in every line.

ROCKY: (ENTERS WITH FLASHLIGHT) Who dat?

ZACKY: Is me, Bredda Zacky.

ROCKY: Bredda Zacky who?

ZACKY: Zachariah from the Church of the Greater Healing of Providence.

ROCKY: Yuh mean obeah man Zacky. What you doing in these parts? (THEY GREET)

ZACKY: I'm tired to tell unno say I am no obeah man. I am a professional prayer warrior. Miss Beatrice send call me to help with a little problem she's having in the district.

ROCKY: Damn idiot dem. Claim say dem see duppy about di place. Moses saw Sally one night and swore it was a rolling calf.

ZACKY: Yuh still a walk and search fah dat old cow?

ROCKY:	She left di pasture and found her way up to Mass Gilbert's property, but she's tied up secured now.
ZACKY:	Sally di rolling calf. Wait deh Rocky. How yuh would a like to have nuff land so yuh don't have to carry her on nobody property to feed?
ROCKY:	Call the word Zacky. Because things harder since Ol' Mammie dead and they fenced off the land that stretches from the church yard to teacher's house.
ZACKY:	Good cigar. Well if things go my way, you and I could own di whole of the land. You could a have money to buy you own fleet of mini-bus and put the government out of business. I can see it...."Rocky's Express Metropolitan Bus". Money, money, money and more money.
ROCKY:	What are you talking about Zacky? Yuh mad or what? Don't involve me into thiefness.
ZACKY:	Theif? I am clean. I have a plan.
ROCKY:	Let me hear it.
ZACKY:	We will put the old cow Sally, to work.
ROCKY:	What kind a work you have in mind?
ZACKY:	Simple. Follow my instructions. I want yuh to put on a heavy chain on di cow with a big bell tied on to the end. Then bring her the churchyard later tonight and let her loose. You should get there bout ten o' clock.
ROCKY:	Moses will run thinking its a rolling calf.
ZACKY:	That is exactly what I want him to do. If we can convince dem, I can get him to sign over di property to di two of us. What you say?

ROCKY: Sounds easy to me. Yuh think dat can work Bredda Zacky?

ZACKY: Well you go on till I get things organized on this end. Set Sally loose and come back to meet me here later. Alright.

ROCKY: All set Bredda Zacky. (EXITS LAUGHING) Sally a go make dem fall-ee-tee.

ZACKY: (ALONE) Mammie, you're my saving grace. If this little plan goes right, I will soon own all the land, house and valuables what you died and left behind. Dead-lef.

BLACK-OUT

ACT I, SCENE 9

NINE NIGHT IN BEATRICE'S YARD. LATE NIGHT. THE VILLAGERS ARE GATHERED LED BY BROTHER ZACKY IS IN A TRANCE. HE LEADS THE GROUP IN A GENERAL IMPROVISED CALL-AND-RESPONSE SINGING AND DANCING SESSION. BEATRICE AND CLARA HOLD BOTTLE TORCHES WHILE MOSES HUGS ON TO HIS BIBLE. ZACKY STANDS BEHIND A TABLE LADEN WITH HUGE DUCK BREADS, SEVERAL BOTTLES OF WHITE RUM, LARGE CANDLES IN SAUCERS AND A NUMBER OF GLASSES WITH WATER, SOME WITH PIECES OF CROTON PLANTS. THE OTHERS SIT ON LONG BENCHES. ROCKY AND CLARA SPEAK UNDER THE SINGING, CHANTING AND HUMMING.

VILLAGERS:	(HYMN LED BY MISS BEATRICE)
	I must have the Savior with me,
	For I dare not go alone,
	I must feel His presence near me,
	And His arm around me thrown.
	Then my soul shall fear no ill, fear no ill,
	Let Him lead me where He will, where He will,
	I will go without a murmur,
	And His footsteps follow still.
ZACKY:	Children of Johoviah, we are gathered in our small number to give thanks fah di life of Mrs. Mammie McIntosh. Together we will lift up di powers of di mighty one and defeat evil. Unno ready to win di battle?
VILLAGERS:	Yes Bredda Zacky.
ZACKY:	Can Satan beat us tonight?
CLARA:	No. Not at all.

43

ZACKY:	Who Bamboo Belly belong to?
VILLAGERS:	We.
ZACKY:	We ready to take it back?
BEATRICE:	Moses, yuh have di ring? You carried di guard ring?
MOSES:	Yes mam. It is wrapped up in a piece of cloth mam.
BEATRICE:	Hold on to it. Just in case Mammie's duppy want to pass through, she must see di ring and take it if she want.
MOSES:	But Miss Beatrice. (PRAYS) The Lord is my shepherd…
CLARA:	Shut yuh mouth with your coward self. When you did a thief di ring you never afraid? Me want a grandstand seat to see di duppy, make I move up further yah.
BEATRICE:	See some a di rice water here Clara, wash yuh face. HANDS CLARA A BOWL)
CLARA:	What is this for Miss Beatrice?
BEATRICE:	Rice water will make yuh see duppy clearer. By the way, where is Goody? Has anybody seen Goody?
CLARA:	Nobody no see her from evening. She has no interest in di dutty ol' bruk dem. Me will take her share of di dead-lef if she no show up yuh know. Me no have no shame.
MOSES:	(STILL PRAYING) Our father which art in heaven…
ZACKY:	Spirit in di air. Brother Moses is pulling dem out.

CLARA:	Geezam peas. Ah what dem dere Miss Beatrice. (SHE POINTS TO SEVERAL GHOST-LIKE IMAGES IN THE AIR)
BEATRICE:	Duppy Clara. All di duppy dem wake up.
CLARA:	No Miss Beatrice, is nothing but dem pickney from down a square a play fool with me.
BEATRICE:	Look, they're dancing. Anything can happen now.
CLARA:	Me never see duppy do dem modern dances yet.
ZACKY:	(CHANTING) Unno come out, all a unno come out a Bamboo Belly district.

CLARA SCREAMS AND FALLS TO THE GROUND.

BEATRICE:	Is what? Clara, is what? Yuh see something?
CLARA:	Is one cockroach run on me foot. Mi frightened, ah thought it was di duppy hold on on me foot.
MOSES:	The Lord is my light and my salvation, whom shall I fear? The Lord is the strength of my life of whom shall I be afraid? When the wicked, even mine enemies and my foes came upon me to eat up my flesh, they stumble and fell...

THERE IS A SPECTACULAR FLASH OF LIGHT. A BULL-LIKE CREATURE APPEARS ON THE VERANDAH. IT IS A ROLLING CALF WITH BLAZING RED EYES WITH FIRE AND SMOKE GASHING FROM ITS NOSTRILS. AS IT ROLLS AROUND THE YARD, IT DRAGS A CHAIN WITH A HUGE BELL MAKING AN UNNERVING CLANKING NOISE. THE SCARED VILLAGERS GRAB ON TO EACH OTHER IN A TIGHT CUDDLE. MOSES FALLS UNCONSCIOUSLY TO THE GROUND.

BEATRICE:	(HOLDS MOSES) Moses, Moses. Get up Moses. Talk to me Moses, talk. Moses naah talk at all. Di duppy box Moses and dumb him.

CURTAIN

ACT TWO

ACT II, SCENE 1

EARLY MORNING. NO CHANGE IN SETTING. BEATRICE WATCHES OVER A MOTIONLESS MOSES WHO LIES ON A BENCH AT ONE CORNER OF THE VERANDAH. THERE IS A LARGE BATH PAN WITH STEAMING HOT WATER. AS THE LIGHTS COME UP, BEATRICE IS POURING LIQUIDS FROM VARIOUS BOTTLES INTO THE PAN. CLARA STANDS TO THE OTHER CORNER OF THE VERANDAH ADDRESSING A CROWD OF VILLAGERS GATHERED OUTSIDE.

CLARA:	Nobody more inquisitive like Bamboo Belly sketel dem. Look deh Miss Beatrice, everybody and dem dog line di fence like dem a wait fah float parade. (TO CROWD) What unno want? Unno never see somebody faint away yet? Hey you, yuh don't have pot on fire? Go on to you yard go feed yuh bang-belly pickney dem and come out a di lady business. So you want to see duppy? See Duppy under you arm. Go away, yuh nose tear out like di rolling calf what you a chat bout. Clear off, make a come out there and you see wrenk and facety.
BEATRICE:	Leave dem alone Clara. They mean no harm.
CLARA:	Yuh want me go out there and sweep dem from in front of you yard mam?

BEATRICE:	No Clara. There is more important things in here to do. Come help me prepare di bath fah Moses.
CLARA:	You a go bathe Moses inna dat? You sure hell-heva Moses can hold in dat little bath pan Miss Beatrice? Is what you put inna di water mam? It smells bad.
BEATRICE:	Dis medicine will cut di crosses. I prepared it myself. It always works. After dis he will be better.
CLARA:	Be careful of these superstition things Miss Beatrice. It's the same thing which killed Mammie. Let us carry Moses to a doctor.
BEATRICE:	No university doctor can cure dis one Clara. No real-real doctor prescription can help Moses now. He needs bush. We need a bush doctor.
CLARA:	What's wrong with you Miss Beatrice? Any doctor can handle a little bad feeling and body-come-down. Is faint way him faint way so lick him head and knock out.
BEATRICE:	That's no faint Clara. The duppy slapped him. Mammie duppy boxed him down and dumb him. Doctors can't heal that.
CLARA:	Nothing like that ma'am. Why would Moses' mother hit him like that?
BEATRICE:	I couldn't answer dat one. But I am sure you was out there and see di rolling calf with you two eye dem. You want more proof than dat?
CLARA:	At least something shut him up fah once. I'm tired of hearing him a neggae-neggae in me ears.
BEATRICE:	Don't make fun of Moses now Clara, he could be dead.

CLARA: Well if you say Bredda Zacky is so good, why you don't make him resurrect Moses? What him out a door a do so long?

BEATRICE: He is sprinkling di yard and burning little incense at all four corners of di house to protect us against the evil spirits.

CLARA: I am tired to tell yuh Miss B, I don't really believe in duppy stories yuh know mam. I only come up here to help out because of you.

BEATRICE: Nobody asking you to believe Clara. But be careful because duppies are real. There are duppies roaming the streets and nothing is worst than a country duppy.

CLARA: Don't make me laugh Miss B. So, you have country duppy separate from town duppy?

BEATRICE: Yes. And country duppy is di worst kind. They are smarter and harder to catch.

CLARA: So what about di town duppy dem?

BEATRICE: A town duppy only frightens people. A country duppy on the other hand torments and takes set on yuh. But nutten takes set like a coolie country duppy.

CLARA: Any duppy ever take set on you yet mam?

BEATRICE: No, but it's not the first time this happened in Bamboo Belly. Long ago there was a little miss who got boxed-down by her sister's duppy because she go deh with di sister's husband two days after her sister died. She's still crazy and walks the streets of Kingston.

CLARA: Serve her right. She didn't need obeah to counteract dat duppy, di sister should a just crab out her eye. She's too brazen.

BEATRICE:	So you see Clara, it's a long time that duppies have been roaming Bamboo Belly.
CLARA:	Well it's not going to catch me ma'am. That is why I am going to give dis place a break. As soon as things work out fah me I am gone to farrin.
BEATRICE:	You don't tired of the American embassy people dem turn you down Clara?
CLARA:	America is not di only place Miss B. There is Canada, England and if worse comes to worse, me will try fah Cayman. Me a go back a Kingston in di week and try fah di Canada visa dis time. Hear say dem a look domestic over deh.
BEATRICE:	You a go leave Bamboo Belly and go do domestic Clara? You who refuse to even wash yu own dutty clothes.
CLARA:	Nobody nah see me over deh mam. And furthermore, the Canadian dollar is stronger than the 'Merican dollar.
ZACKY:	(ENTERING) Seal and sign. Miss Beatrice, no spirits will ever enter your house again. Di bath looks like it ready now. We better start before it gets too cold after which it is of no use.
BEATRICE:	One more thing. Clara, look on di table inna di kitchen yuh see some lime. Cut a few a dem bring come. (CLARA GOES OFF)
CLARA:	How many limes yuh want?
BEATRICE:	Enough to squeeze in di bath, plus to rub him up after.
CLARA:	Mind unno kill Moses. A tell yuh to call Dr. Lewis ma'am.

ZACKY:	Dis is higher science than doctor science.
BEATRICE:	What else is going into di bath Brother Zacky?
ZACKY:	Nothing chases off spirits like Rosemary bush Sister B. You have leaf-of-life? Mix it with little High-John-the-Conqueror weed and that will be alright. But you know nothing can work until you settle di bill.
BEATRICE:	How much me owe yuh Bredda Zacky?
ZACKY:	You owe me nothing Sister. Consider it a donation to the work of the Lord and the Church of the Greater Healing of Providence. That will be five hundred U.S.
BEATRICE:	U.S. dollars? What Bredda Zacky? Where should I get US dollars from? After me not running a Cambio up here?
ZACKY:	Shame on you Sister B. All other transaction in dis country is in US dollars, why you think di work of di Lord is any different? Furthermore I also have me overseas commitment.
CLARA:	DeLawrence. Careful of DeLawrence ma'am.
ZACKY:	Careful what yuh saying sister. Local prayer warriors don't need farrin assistance. Miss Beatrice, yuh want to get rid of dis duppy or what?
BEATRICE:	Yes, Bredda Zacky. See di money here. I'm doing this only for the sake of poor Moses.
CLARA:	(RETURNS WITH LIMES) What unno whispering for?
BEATRICE:	Nothing Clara. Help me squeeze di limes into di pan.

ZACKY: And dat is not all Sister Beatrice, drop di balance of these oils in di bath. (HE HANDS BEATRICE A FEW VIALS OF COLOURED LIQUIDS. SHE OPENS AND POURS ONE AT A TIME) When di bath finish, send somebody go to sea with a zinc pan and fetch some sea water. Then pour some of the oil in it and use di mixture to wash di floor around di bed which he will sleep on tonight. One thing, whatever water is left back, you are to return it to di sea. And on your way back from di seaside, speak to no one, and don't ever look back.

BEATRICE: OK Brother Zacky, I will try to remember all of that. Di bath look good now. Come, unno help me sit him up over it.

BEATRICE PLACES A PLANK OF WOOD ACROSS THE RIM OF THE BATH PAN. THEY ALL ASSIST IN SEATING MOSES OVER THE PAN. BREDDA ZACKY APPLIES A MIXTURE TO MOSES'S HEAD AND USES A TOWEL TO SPONGE HIS BACK AND ARMS. SUDDENLY, MOSES JUMPS AS IF A SPIRIT BEING EXORCIZED. HE SPEAKS IN TONGUES AND HAS TO BE HELD DOWN BY THE OTHERS.

ZACKY: Sister B, unno grab him quick. Di spirit is escaping. Quick, Clara, pass di pint bottle. (CLARA FETCHES AN EMPTY SODA BOTTLE) Di duppy is getting away. (HE RUNS AROUND IN A CHASE) Me catch her, me catch di duppy. (HE HOLDS UP THE BOTTLE TO THE SKY AND CORKS IT BRISKLY)

MOSES: Forgive me Lord, for I know not what I do. Me never mean to do it Lord. Lord me sorry Lord.

BEATRICE: (STILL TRYING TO HOLD HIM DOWN) Do what? What yuh talking about Moses?

MOSES: Is me do it, is me do it.

CLARA:	He is getting mad now. He is talking stupidness. Unno call Bellevue Hospital.
BEATRICE:	Hold on to him Clara. Don't let him get away.
ZACKY:	(SPEAKS IN TONGUES) Peace be still. Speak it sister. Everything alright now, I have di spirit right here so. Away with evil spirits. All me have to do now is fling dis bottle go a sea and that's di end of Ol' Mammie duppy.
MOSES:	(CRYING) Lord, if ah know she was going to come after me, I wouldn't do it. Me sorry Miss Beatrice, me really sorry mam.
BEATRICE:	Sorry fah what Moses? What yuh do?
MOSES:	Di will mam. Is me put me name on di will. Unno don't bother call di police, ah beg unno please mam.
BEATRICE:	Yuh not making sense Moses.
MOSES:	Me change it mam. When me find di will me just shut me eye and draw me name on it mam.
BEATRICE:	Whose name was on it Moses? Who did Mammie leave di property for?
MOSES:	Goody ma'am. She lef every jack thing to dat woman name Goody. That not fair Miss Beatrice. Look how I nursed Mammie in her sick bed?
BEATRICE:	So what you do with di will?
MOSES:	Me give it to Bredda Zacky mam, me never touch nothing else mam. Kiss di cross and cross me heart mam. Don't it Bredda Zacky, me give you it sir?
ZACKY:	True Sister Beatrice. I have it. So tell me, Goody is di rightful inheritor of di dead-lef things? Goody her pickney. Dat is Good

MOSES: Yes Bredda Zacky. Goody got everything sir. Well sir, me say me not leaving and no get someting too. Dat was when I took di guard ring too. I am really sorry mam. Ah pray to massa God fah forgiveness. See di ring here mam, take it, ah don't want anything to do with her mam. Take it mam, take di ring.

MISS BEATRICE AND ZACKY PULL AWAY. CLARA LOOKS AT THEM, TAKES A BEAT THEN SLOWLY PULLS OFF THE RING FROM MOSES' FINGER, SHE ADMIRES IT AND GENTLY PLACES IT ON HER FINGER.

                                                    BLACK-OUT

ACT II, SCENE 2

ZACKY AND ROCKY MEET OUTSIDE IN THE YARD TO THE SIDE OF BEATRICE'S HOUSE.

ROCKY:	Brother Zacky, ah tired to search fah you. Ah want to see you long time. Things are not right.
ZACKY:	Everything is under control. No need to be nervous. Look what I make in one day's work already. Five hundred US dollars. And I am not done as yet; I still have more to collect.
ROCKY:	But Brother Zacky, things are not the way they seem.
ZACKY:	No need to fret Rocky, you will get your rightful share out of di runnings. By di time I am done with them, everybody will empty their bank accounts. Dis money is from Beatrice. I get to understand dat Moses is sitting on a fat bank account. I am sure he will want protection from di rest of spirits that I will to set on him.
ROCKY:	I heard he saw a rolling calf and Mammie duppy slapped the senses out from him.
ZACKY:	(LAUGHS) He has been telling people. But you and I know how di rolling calf story goes already. My apprentice Rocky, you were good fah true. It looked so real, I myself was also afraid.
ROCKY:	Dats what I wanted to talk to you about Bredda Zacky.

ZACKY:	Dat was perfect. You should have seen their face when it appeared. Everybody was frightened. Well in all di excitement, Moses dropped and swore di duppy box him down. He claims that Ol' Mammie possessed him. Well dat was more work and more money for yours truly. Here is the bottle, I told them that I captured it and will cast it away at sea. There is only one problem in this plan.
ROCKY:	What is dat?
ZACKY:	The will is a bogus will. Moses confessed that he forged it and wrote his own name on it.
ROCKY:	So what are we going to do? How di payment a go? All I am concerned about now is my payments, my money Bredda Zacky.
ZACKY:	Don't worry Rocky, me have di money business under control. Yuh safe man, yuh safer than a bulla in a glass case.
ROCKY:	And what about the will? Whose name is on it? She must lef di things dem fah her daughter in farrin.
ZACKY:	If its di daughter Goody who got the inheritance, then we have no problem. (LAUGHS) Cause yuh and I know say I know Goody very well. Miss Beatrice is going to get di original from JP. Di little plan with Sally yuh cow work fine so noting cyan stop we from working another show.
ROCKY:	Dat is what ah want to tell yuh long time. Di thing what unno see di other night was not Sally.

ZACKY: What yuh chatting say? Yuh joking fah true. I took me own two eyes and saw when Sally jumped up on dah verandah. I had to pretend like I was also afraid so no one would get suspicious. Our rolling calf Sally made dem feneh yuh see. Sally di rolling calf.

ROCKY: Rolling calf yes Bredda Zacky, but it wasn't my cow Sally unno see. Me collect Sally from pasture early in di evening as me promise, but river come down and flooded the place so I couldn't cross over to get to the church. Me and Sally spent all night over di river bank. Bredda Zacky, its only this morning before I could cross di river and come over.

ZACKY: Well if dat wasn't Sally, what was dat creature which appeared on Miss Beatrice's verandah last night? Karamba. Crosses.

ROCKY: What yuh asking me dat for? Me no know a what unno see? I wasn't there.

ZACKY: Looks like there is a real-real duppy in Bamboo Belly fah true.

ROCKY: (SCARED) If that was a real duppy, so what is that you caught in the bottle you have in your hand?

ZACKY: Blow-wow. Yuh mean say is a real-real duppy dis inna di bottle? A real live duppy? (HE HOLDS UP THE BOTTLE) Mammie duppy come back to rahtid.

ZACKY THROWS THE BOTTLE TO ROCKY. HE RETURNS IT. THEY TOSS IT AROUND. THE BOTTLE FALLS AND BREAKS. SWIFT EXIT.

BLACK-OUT

ACT II, SCENE 3

BEATRICE'S YARD. ZACKY ENTERS AND CLOSES THE GATE BEHIND HIM. ZACKY IS AFRAID. HE STANDS WITH HIS BACK TO THE GATE FOR A WHILE THEN CHECKS TO SEE IF HE IS BEING FOLLOWED. HE SIGHS ALOUD AND IS SURPRISED BY BEATRICE AS SHE ENTERS FROM HER ROOM.

BEATRICE:	You get rid of di duppy brother Zacky?
ZACKY:	(STARTLED) Duppy, which duppy? Another duppy? Where it deh? Away evil spirits. Away.
BEATRICE:	Is Mammie duppy me a talk, what you catch in di pint bottle. Why are you sweating?
ZACKY:	No reason mam. I got rid of Mammie duppy long time ago. She is now swimming with fish in the Caribbean sea.
BEATRICE:	I hope so. Shark will nyam her and full dem belly.
ZACKY:	Come make we move fast with di other things dem. Di quicker we read di correct will and give everybody what they are supposed to get is di better it is for everyone. Furthermore I have another appointment in St. Thomas.
BEATRICE:	Why yuh rushing Bredda Zacky? Nobody going to thief you.
ZACKY:	Taking bout dat, I want some more down payment.
BEATRICE:	How much more you want?
ZACKY:	Another five hundred more in US.

BEATRICE:	Well seeing that the reading of the will is not my business, what I will do is inform Miss Goody and Moses. They said that they are family and it looks like Goody got the bulk of inheritance so we can't proceed till she come.
ZACKY:	Well guess what, yuh don't need Miss Goody. We can do without her.
BEATRICE:	I sent somebody go call her already. She is family, this is really her business.
ZACKY:	No. Don't call her. She's not to come up here until the will is read. She is not a believer so she will only hamper progress. Furthermore, we can't gurantee dat anything is in the will for her. Next thing she gets on bad and mash up di place.

THERE IS A BANGING ON THE ROOF. MOSES ENTERS FROM BEDROOM.

MOSES:	Listen, that's Mammie's duppy again Miss Beatrice, listen to her.
ZACKY:	Where is she? Away, Away.
BEATRICE:	Nothing like tha Moses. Brother Zacky trapped her and throw her into the sea a long time ago. Right now she is helping to stir up hurricanes.
ZACKY:	Exactly so. Next storm coming to Jamaica will be called Hurricane Mammie.
MOSES:	So what is that tapping sound that we hear on top of the house? Mammie is guarding di place until di will is read.
BEATRICE:	The sooner we read the will, the sooner she will go about her business.

ZACKY:	Miss Beatrice, since di will was tampered with, why don't we just make a list of everything Mammie owned and share it up evenly between all of us? That way nobody gets left out. I will take the haunted house.
MOSES:	Yuh mad or what? How you come into dis? How you come to business into we business? How comes yuh want to claim the house?
BEATRICE:	That was only an idea Moses.
MOSES:	I don't like di sound of this Miss Beatrice. Something is funny about Bredda Zacky mam. (SOUNDS ON ROOF) Hear Mammie deh again. It's a sign. Everytime she lick di roof, dat means something not right.
BEATRICE:	Moses, nobody will thief anything from you and Goody. Furthermore I collected the original will from JP Ferguson. Ah have it right here. It don't even open yet.
ZACKY:	Well, let's do what we have to do. And do it quick. Where's di rest of di people?
MOSES:	Yes, where is Clara? Where is my lovely sister Goody? I want to be with her to share the joy.
BEATRICE:	Clara is gone to the bend-down market in Falmouth. And your sister Goody will be here shortly.
ZACKY:	Keep Goody away, she is not to come inside di house. Di spirit no flush out properly yet. We don't need her right away. Where is the will? Let us look at it now.
BEATRICE:	No Bredda Zacky. I won't open it without one of Mammie relatives present. We can get in trouble with di law. Fraud is a serious thing yuh know Bredda Zacky and me nah go a prison fah people money.

59

ZACKY: All right Miss Beatrice. So where is she? If she dont come soon we'll have to go on with the proceedings.

BEATRICE: She is coming Bredda Zacky. Me send message to di hotel where she staying telling her to come quick to hear di will.

ZACKY: Well, tell yuh what, I will volunteer to go to her. I will meet her part way and personally escort her back up here so we can explicate di will without any delay whatsoever.

BEATRICE: Bredda Zacky yuh don't have to do all a that yuh know.

ZACKY: No problem Sister, whenever I have work to do, I always make sure it is complete.

BEATRICE: All right den. Hurry Bredda Zacky bcause we have to read di will today. (MISS BEATRICE ESCORTS ZACKY TO THE GATE. HE WALKS DOWN THE STREET) Make haste. (TO MOSES) Take you cloth off my machine!

BLACK-OUT

ACT II, SCENE 4

SAME SETTING AS BEFORE. BEATRICE AND MOSES ARE ON THE
VERANDAH WHEN 'GOODY' ENTERS.

GOODY: Hallooo.......Halloooooo. It's only me, Goody mam. Did I miss di will? I come as fast as I hear say di will find. Miss Beatrice, here is my birth clarification. See I am a literated child of Miss Mammie McIntosh.

BEATRICE: Is alright Goody, you don't have to prove nothing me love. Moses already confessed.

GOODY: Well to tell di truth man, I heard a little gossip on on my way up here. (TO MOSES) Imagine Moses, all dat just fah little dead lef things? I will set you up on something after I collect the inheritance.

MOSES: Don't bother sorry fah me. (POINTS TO THE SKY) See my provider up dere. Him will look after me yuh hear Miss Goody.

BEATRICE: Goody, you sit over deh so. We almost ready to read di will. Mass Zacky is gone down the road to look fah you. He will soon be back.

GOODY: Oh I saw him in di sqaure. He said we should go ahead with di will cause he has to go back to Falmouth for business. So let us proceed wid di procession. You have di will? Who got it? Where is it? Let us proceed.

BEATRICE OPENS THE ENVELOPE. THERE IS A LOUD BANG ON
THE ROOF.

MOSES: Hear Mammie deh again, she is warning us again.

GOODY: Warn us fah what? Why would she want to warn us now that we solved di problem? Dat duppy is an evil spirit.

MOSES: Mammie is not an evil spirit. Mammie duppy was a good duppy like di one dem what protect yuh.

BEATRICE That being the case, she is only back to watch over the reading of the will. Well the quicker we read it is the quicker she can go on about her business. (READS) *"I, Mammie Preticia Adassa McIntosh, in the presence of JP Claudius Ferguson in the parish of St. James in Jamaica West Indies, do hereby leave the following things to the following people. The pot set and crockery to Teacher Patterson, because she loves to eat. All the jewelry, rings, chains, broaches to Miss Clara because only she can wear them nice."*

MOSES: Saviour divine, Miss Beatrice, are you sure you saw Miss Clara's name?

BEATRICE: Bright as daylight. Clara Mitchell. Well judging from what I am seeing, Mammie was generous fah true. She know Clara used to block her all di time and yet still she remember her.

MOSES: Nutten there fah me Miss Beatrice?

BEATRICE: Ah still reading. (SHE CONTINUES READING) *"The piece of land running from the cotton tree to the church plus the lovely five bedroom house together with three cows and seven goats to my one and only pickney Goody."* But dere is more...

GOODY: (CRYING) Oh thanks Mammie, thanks to you mam. Where is di title? And unno think dat I was telling a lie all dis time.

BEATRICE:	Hold on dere Miss Goody. Me say more deh here. *"The shop and all me money in me bank book to Brother Zacky."* But dat is strange, even Bredda Zacky fared out good out a dis one.
MOSES:	Forger. Someting isn't right about dat. When I first saw it, nothing was left fah Bredda Zacky.
GOODY:	Are you contesting the legality of the will that my mother and di JP signed together?
MOSES:	Miss Beatrice, if its one thing me did do when me did a look on di will mam, is read. And as far as me member, di shop and her money did leave to her church. And Mammie was not a member of Bredda Zacky's church.
CLARA:	(ENTERS DRUNK) Where she is? Where is di woman name Goody? Where is she Miss Beatrice? Hold on to her. (TO GOODY) Hello Miss, I would a like to have a word with yuh. Just a word.
GOODY:	What is di problem lady? Why are you looking at me in dat tone of voice?
CLARA:	Ah don't look on you yet. You ever see prison yet?
GOODY:	What? Listen to me Miss Beatrice I shall be running soon yuh hear. Unno can read di will without me. In di morning, I will pick up whatever Mammie lef fah me. (SHE TRIES TO LEAVE)
CLARA:	(BLOCKING GOODY) Don't let her leave the yard Miss Beatrice. She can tell you about the tapping sounds on your roof top.
BEATRICE:	What sound Clara? What you talking bout?

CLARA:	All di banging and commotion on your roof every day.
BEATRICE:	Hopefully dat was di last of Mammie. Bredda Zacky said he fixed it so the banging sound will stop now.
CLARA:	Fix what? Dat had nothing to do with Mammie. That was the bang-gut pickney dem from up di hill who were stoning your mango tree. Me had to runchase them away just now. I see Leena big foot bway a run up and down on di raw zinc roof.
BEATRICE:	So it was di pickney dem I heard on the roof and thought it was Mammie's duppy?
CLARA:	Me tell unno long time say nothing no go so. Ask Miss Goody, she knows bout it too. She is involved.
GOODY:	Involved with what mam? Miss Clara, be careful that you don't obstruct di work of di powers of righteousness.
CLARA:	Powers? Beatrice, I hope yuh never give any money to dis thiefing obeah man Zacky yuh know. Him is a criminal. The police in Falmouth looking fah him.
GOODY:	Sister Beatrice, I will venture up to Bredda Zacky house right away and make sure him come down here and explain it to di whole a unno.
CLARA:	Whey you a go Miss Tufness? (HOLDS ON TO GOODY) How yuh know where Bredda Zacky lives? Do you know Falmouth?

GOODY:	How yuh mean if I know Falmouth? Is there I born and grow. Well it reminds me of the U.S. Bredda Zacky have the big white house on the hill, with the flag dem, six red flag, two green and one gold, and the cross paint on the gate. Ah gone go catch him, me can't stop.
BEATRICE:	Let her go.
CLARA:	(RELEASES GOODY) Miss Beatrice, you shouldn't make her get away. Me catch dat news at di square today. Unno always tease me about rum, but thanks to rum, me get di full Bamboo Belly duppy story.
BEATRICE:	Story? Duppy story? What story you talking about Clara?
CLARA:	It's a long story Miss Beatrice. Well, Rocky and I were at the bar drinking rum. And you know that he can't hold his liquor. So he started to talk a lot of things about how Bredda Zacky promises him money. According to him, Bredda Zacky rented his cow and dressed it up so as to frighten all of us here at the nine night. Well at the same time Zacky dressed up as a woman named Goody so he could get Mammie's inheritance.
BEATRICE:	So, that ugly thiefing Zacky and the tough mampie Goody is one and the same person. Watch me and dem tonight.

BLACK-OUT

ACT II, SCENE 5

MISS BEATRICE YARD. LATE EVENING. MISS BEATRICE IS EXPECTING A VISIT FROM GOODY. MOSES IS PRETENDING TO BE 'POSSESSED' ONCE MORE BY MAMMIE'S DUPPY AS MISS BEATRICE TRIES SOME CREATIVE REMEDIES.

GOODY:	(ENTERING) Halloooo, hallooooo. Miss Beatice? Miss Beatrice? What is the matter mam? As I heard yuh send call me I hurry up and come. Is Moses ill? Is he possessed again mam?
MOSES:	(LOUD BAWLING) Miss Beatrice, me ah dead.
BEATRICE:	(WHISPERS) Moses, yuh are to bawl like its real. That doesn't sound convincing enough. Bawl some more.
MOSES:	(HE TALKS LIKE MAMMIE) Oh Bamboo belly people, free me. Set me free from dis body.
BEATRICE:	Goody my child, you wouldn't understand. Mammie duppy has returned. Poor Moses, he got hit again.
GOODY:	But how did it come back? I am sure that Bredda Zacky exorcised the spirit already.
BEATRICE:	Mammie's duppy is a devil of a duppy Goody. Dis time she came back with a vengeance and she is giving plenty warning too. But I have her under control.
MOSES:	(SPEAKS LIKE MAMMIE) Deceiver, trickster and imposter. Liar, criminal and thief.
GOODY:	Miss Beatrice, it seems like Moses is illuminating mam. All I am here for is my inheritance, so dat me can leave Bamboo Belly in the morning.

BEATRICE:	We going to continue to read the will Goody. But Mammie says we must wait a little, listen to her talk.
MOSES:	(AS MAMMIE) They are coming to rob Bamboo Belly. Look to the left, look to the right. Look in the white house on the hill with the flags, six red flag, two green and one gold, and the cross painted on the gate. Listen to me and follow me.
BEATRICE:	Listen to Mammie. Do you know that house Goody?
GOODY:	Not at all Miss Beatrice. Not at all. What does she say we are to do?
MOSES:	(HOLDS ON TO GOODY) Divest your garments and lay them on the tabernacle and peace will be with you forever. Spin around ten times. Turn to di right, turn to the left and kneel down.
BEATRICE:	Do what she says. (BEATRICE REMOVES HER HEAD TIE AND SHOES) Come Goody, she says you are to take off yuh clothes, you must follow me. Do it.

GOODY SLOWLY TAKES OFF HER CLOTHES AND FOLLOWS THE INSTRUCTIONS OF 'MAMMIE'. SHE IS SCARED.

GOODY:	Miss Beatrice. Dis duppy business getting too far now. There is no such thing. Moses, stop di foolishness. (REMOVES HAT AND VEIL TO REAVEAL HERSELF AS ZACKY)
BEATRICE:	(STARES) Bredda Zacky, is that you? What are you doing dressed up like this? The frock fits you fah sure. (ZACKY TRIES TO GO) Moses, hold on to him.

ZACKY: It was just for the money Miss Beatrice. I heard dat Mammie left a large inheritance fah Goody and since there was no Goody to claim it, I thought that I could claim it on behalf of my church on di hill.

BEATRICE: Why yuh so lie Zacky? Did you think that we are all idiots here in Bamboo Belly? You have more nerve than a rotten tooth. Imagine, you came into our village to take advantage of us. The police will fix you.

ZACKY: Police, what police have to do with dis Miss Beatrice?

BEATRICE: You are a fraud.

ZACKY: Miss Beatrice, I was only trying to help.

BEATRICE: Den how come yuh take me money? Well where is me money?

ZACKY: Dat was for di ingredients in di bath Sister Beatrice.

BEATRICE: Where is my five hundred US dollars?

ZACKY: Ah have it right here. See it here mam. (RETURNS MONEY) I must go now mam. (HE MOVES AWAY WITHOUT NOTICING CLARA)

CLARA: Boo. (CLARA ENTERS AND FRIGHTENS ZACKY WHO RUNS AND JUMPS OVER THE FENCE AND HEADS DOWN THE ROAD) Ha ha ha. Miss Beatrice, yuh see when him, she or shim scale di fence. (LAUGHS) Yuh read the will yet Miss B?

BEATRICE: If mi read di will? Mi read it so many times, till mi read di bogus one too. But something else, there is another sheet of paper that I didn't get to read. See it here. It is someone's birth certificate.

CLARA:	Whose is it?
BEATRICE:	Dis look like. (SHE READS ALOUD) "*Moses Goody McIntosh.*" Its Moses' birth certificate. (READS) "*The male child of Mammie McIntosh born on this day, stamped Registrar General, Government of Jamaica.*"
CLARA:	Moses Goody McIntosh? Can someone have a name like that? Moses ah Mammie pickney?
BEATRICE:	Goody? Moses? Moses, your name is Goody. You are really Mammie's pickney.
MOSES:	Is dat me a try to tell unno long time. Is dat Mammie did a whisper tell me on her dead bed. So she said - *Moses, Goody. Moses, Goody.*
CLARA:	(EXCITED) Moses, you know say me and you are friends long time. We have to celebrate together. Share and share alike. What yuh say Moses?
BEATRICE:	As long as you willing to share your piece of di legacy Clara. Because yuh know say your name is on the will too.
CLARA:	Story. Make me see it fah me self. (SHE READS) "*Gold chain and gold ring.*" Blouse and kkirt, me rich. Who want to buy dem? Ah need di money to buy me ticket.
BEATRICE:	Ticket to go where?
CLARA:	Ah get it Beatrice. Finally. (HOLDS UP PASSPORT) Me finally get di visa mam.
BEATRICE:	Wait, but dem don't have no embassy in Falmouth? How you get visa a Falmouth?
CLARA:	Connections. Its not only in Kingston you can buy a visa in Jamaica. Finally ah going to leave dis backward place.
BEATRICE:	Yuh cant turn yuh back on us like that.

CLARA:	Watch me and see. Dis is my opportunity to get some progress in my life.
BEATRICE:	So what yuh a go do a farrin?
CLARA:	Well ah don't know yuh know mam. But Marcia said I was to come and try a ting. Dats why mi bring dis piece a material fah yuh mek one coat fah me. (TAKES OUT FABRIC)
BEATRICE:	Listen to me yuh hear Clara. Where Marcia going find place put yuh? She up there for five years now and she isn't yet working. Does Marcia have her green card?
CLARA:	No mam. But she said I am to still come. She sent this piece of cloth for me to make a coat to travel come up to America.
BEATRICE:	Come mek me tek di measurement. Moses, pass di platform come. All right Miss Clara come me tek measurement fah yuh coat. Stand up straight. Yuh want long coat or short coat? Winter coat or spring coat?
CLARA:	Me no know mam. Just one coat mam. Like di one me see on television to keep off di snow.
BEATRICE:	There is no snow in America now Clara, it is summer now. See yuh not even know which part yuh a go. Take my foolish advice and go up there for a visit first before you spread bed. Go see what it is like up there first.
CLARA:	All right mam. But me still want di coat mam. So when me reach in Montego Bay airport me can shock out. (BEATRICE MEASURES). Like how a summer, Miss Beatrce, mek it short up here so.

BEATRICE: No Clara, a winter coat has to cover yuh bottom. (MEASURES WAIST) Stop, yuh waist was thirty-two just the other day and now it is thirty-six. You gone up? Yuh pregnant?

CLARA: Gone up which part Miss Beatrice? You must be mad Miss Beatrice. Me not into dat mam. Is just a little weight me putting on. But don't watch dat Miss Beatrice, still make di waist thirty-two and me will pull in me belly mam.

BEATRICE: Tell yuh what, me will make it loose fitting, so just in case yuh gone up, it will accommodate the expansion. Forty-five.

CLARA: Dat would have to be Banboo Belly first immaculate conception Miss Beatrice. No bother set yuh mout on me yuh hear mam. Miss B, like how a summer, make di coat to catch me here so.

BEATRICE: No Clara, ah say coat to cover yuh bottom.

CLARA: Miss Beatrice, mi can get little fur on di collar? And put some seaquins on di sleve. And Miss B, ah want a bashment scarf to wrap around me neck like dis. (SHE STRIKES A POSE AND SMILES WITH MOSES)

BEATRICE: (SHE SEES THE CONNECTION BETWEEN MOSES AND CLARA AS THEY STARE AT EACH OTHER) Ummmm. Moses reach to di promised land.

CURTAIN

Country Duppy (2000) advertising poster, Barn
Theatre, New Kingston, Jamaica

Miss Beatrice (Leonie Forbes) confronts the duppy in *Country Duppy* (2000)

Clara (Tulip Reid), Moses (Christopher Daley) and Miss
Beatrice (Leonie Forbes) prepare to face the duppy.

Miss Beatrice (Leonie Forbes) reads the will in **Country Duppy** (2000)

Miss Beatrice (Leonie Forbes) measures up Clara
(Tulip Reid) in *Country Duppy* (2000)

Curtain call for Country Duppy (2001) in Toronto with Zacky
(Naggo Morris), Rocky (Elvis Hamilton) Beatrice (Leonie
Forbes), Clara (Marcia Brown) and Moses (Kevin Sinclair)

Actress Leonie Forbes (left) presents flowers to Louise Bennett (Miss Lou) and her husband Eric Coverley following *Country Duppy* (2001) in Toronto

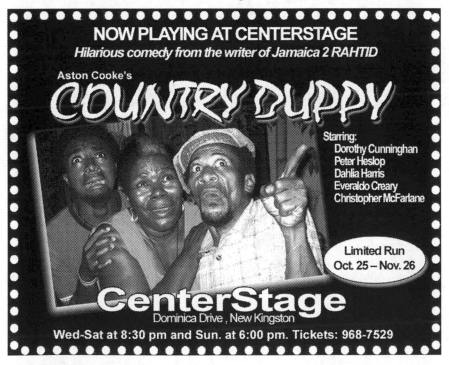

Poster for *Country Duppy* (2007) at Centre Stage Theatre in Kingston

Clara (Dahlia Harris), Beatrice (Dorothy Cunningham) and Moses (Everaldo Creary) in a scene from *Country Duppy* (2007)

Miss Beatrice scolds Moses in *Country Duppy* (2007)

Miss Beatrice (Dorothy Cunningham) greets Brother Zacky (Peter Heslop) while Moses (Everaldo Creary, centre) looks on in *Country Duppy* (2007)

Another scene from the 2007 production of *Country Duppy*

Advertising poster for *Jonkanoo Jamboree* at PSCCA, UWI, Mona (2013)

Set design by Michael Lorde for *Jonkanoo Jamboree*(2013)

Gizzada (Shanique Brown, centre) checks off the money
from the bar in *Jonkanoo Jamboree*(2013)

Shadow (Desmond Dennis) and Clappers (Fabian Thomas)
meet with Mr. Buckingsworth (Brian Johnson)

Gizzada (Shanique Brown) teams up with Stagger Back
(Melbourne Douglas) in *Jonkanoo Jamboree*(2013)

Trevor (Danar Royal) advises his mother Precious (Julene Robinson) in a scene from *Jonkanoo Jamboree*(2013)

Traditional Jonkanoo dancers clash with dancehall
dancers in *Jonkanoo Jamboree*(2013)

Miss Terrylonge (Nadean Rawlings) and her grand daughter
Malika (Shantol Jackson) in *Jonkanoo Jamboree*(2013)

Competition time and the *Jonkanoo Village* dancers perform.

The Finale from *Jonkanoo Jamboree*(2013)

JONKANOO JAMBOREE

First performed by the University Players at the **The Philip Sherlock Centre for the Creative Arts**, University of the West Indies, Jamaica on Friday, October 11, 2013 with the following cast:

Precious	Julene Robinson
Mas Benjamin	Tyane Robinson
Miss Terrylonge	Nadean Rawlins
Malika	Shantol Jackson
Trevor	Danar Royal
Stagger Back	Melbourne Douglas
Gizzada	Shanique Brown
Mas Zacky	Michael Dane Lewis
Mr. Bukingsworth	Brian Johnson
Mrs. Buckingsworth	Shawna Kae Burns
Sarah Buckingsworth	Renae Williams
Adasa	Honica Brown
Joyce	Suzanne Beadle
Mr. Donalds	Andre Bernard
Mrs. Donalds	Susie Braham
Corporal Clappers	Fabian Thomas
Shadow	Desmond Dennis
MC	Romane Duncan
Mada Lundi	N/A
Villagers	Jason Williams, Kemar Brown, Chelsea Brown
	Naala Nesbeth, Aaron Linton, Jourdanne Hart
	Tiffany Thompson

Musicians :	Jhevaughn Murphy, Jon Joseph Nepaul, Andrew Campbell
	Jenoy McKoy

Directed by Michael Holgate

ACT ONE

ACT I, SCENE 1

MID AFTERNOON IN JANKONOO VILLAGE SQUARE. JONKANOO VILLAGE IS A SMALL FISHING VILLAGE SOMEWHERE ON JAMAICA'S COASTLINE. THE VILLAGE IS MADE UP OF SMALL BUT WELL APPOINTED WOODEN HOUSES. THE VILLAGERS' HOMES SURROUND A BIG HOUSE WHICH IS OWNED BY MRS. HYACINTH TERRYLONGE, A LONG STANDING RESIDENT WHO NOW RESIDES ABROAD. ON THE HILL IN THE BACKGROUND IS PROPERTY BELONGING TO MR. BUCKINGSWORTH ON WHICH STANDS THE 'QUADRILLE HEIGHTS RESORT HOTEL'. THERE IS A HISTORY OF COSTUME MAKING IN THE VILLAGE WHICH HAS A JONKANOO DANCING TRADITION. THE JONKANOO TRADITION IS BEING KEPT ALIVE BY MAS BENJAMIN, AN OLD COSTUME MAKER. ITS HOLIDAY TIME AND THE VILLAGERS STILL ENJOY WHAT IS LEFT OF THEIR PROUD BUT DYING JONKANOO TRADITION.

CHILD:	They're coming, they're coming. Jonkanoo ah come. See dem there, the Jonkanoo ah come. Jonkanoo ah come.
PRECIOUS:	Which part dem deh? Where dem reach?
CHILD:	They reach up by schoolyard next to Mas Zacky's property. They're coming, dem ah come. Jonkanoo ah come and ah 'fraid.
VILLAGERS:	(SING)
	Jonkanoo. Jonkanoo. Jonkanoo a come.

Pitchy Patchy leading the Jonkanoo band

Jonkanoo. Jonkanoo. Jonkanoo a come.

Everybody run come, di Jonkanoo a come

Di Jonkanoo band coming up the street

Fife and drum music playing sweet-sweet

Jonkanoo. Jonkanoo. Jonkanoo a come.

Everybody run come, di jonkanoo a come

See Pitchy Patchy, devil and Belly woman

See Horse-head, cow-head and Policeman

Jonkanoo. Jonkanoo. Jonkanoo a come.

Everybody run come, Jonkanoo a come

Join di band mek we jump and prance

Jonkanoo people mek we do Jonkanoo dance

Jonkanoo. Jonkanoo. Jonkanoo a come.

Jonkanoo. Jonkanoo. Jonkanoo a come.

THERE IS EXCITEMENT IN THE VILLAGE AS THE CROWD AWAITS THE JONKANOO PARADE. STAGGER BACK AND GIZZADA ENTER. BOTH ARE OVERDRESSED IN TYPICAL JAMAICAN DANCEHALL OUTFITS RESEMBLING TWO JONKANOO CHARACTERS.

GIZZADA: Yellow tape. Unno never see beauty queen yet?

PRECIOUS: No man. Unno favour Jonkanoo fi true, no wonder di pickney frighten.

STAGGER: Oh so badly.

PRECIOUS: Dat is oh so correct, unno looking so badly.

STAGGER:	Tcho mam, is me Stagger Back you a chat bout? Me is di girl dem serve me long.
GIZZADA:	And me Gizzada. Me sweet like sugar and coconut. We a shock out don't it?
PRECIOUS:	Shock out? Yes. Unno look like lightening strike di two a unno.
TREVOR:	Mama. Just cool nuh man.
GIZZADA:	What ah gwaan Trevor? Yuh good? Yuh look good.
TREVOR:	True?
PRECIOUS:	Trevor, don't look in dat direction.
TREVOR:	Cho Mama man.
GIZZADA:	Miss Precious, me a good girl enuh. And me look good too. Don't Trevor. Me nah go mek di Jonkanoo parade look better than me this year. So you like di outfit mam? (SHE MODELS)
PRECIOUS:	Unno never need no costume fi favour Jonkanoo. See it deh you Pitchy Patchy and you is definitely ass-head.
TREVOR:	Mama, it look like di Jonkanoo band a come now. (LOOKS AT GIZZADA AND STAGGER AND STIFLES A LAUGH) Di real-real Jonkanoo dem a come.

JONKANOO MUSIC OF FIFE AND DRUM IS HEARD IN THE DISTANCE. IT GETS LOUDER AS THE BAND APPROACHES. A SMALL UNIMPRESSIVE LOOKING JONKANOO BAND TREKS ACROSS THE STAGE AND PUTS ON AN EQUALLY UNIMPRESSIVE AND DISAPPOINTING PERFORMANCE.

GIZZADA:	Ah what dat? Which part unno a go wid dat deh fenkeh fenkeh bruk foot heng pon nail dance?

STAGGER:	Ah idiot Jonkanoo dat. (LAUGHS) Hey Gizzada, mek we show dem the latest dance. (THEY IMPROVISE) Give me little riddim. (GIZZADA STARTS CLAPPING AND DANCING TO DANCEHALL MUSIC) Dis one name di Jonkanoo. Chat bout.
BENJAMIN:	Unno don't know nutten bout Jonkanoo. Tell dem Trevor. You know better. This same Jonkanoo is what your grandfather used to dance right here in Jonkanoo Beach Village.
PRECIOUS:	Is Jonkanoo send unno go a school. Jonkanoo made this village.
STAGGER:	Jonkanoo is backwardness. Dancehall run things all over the world now. Tell dem nuh Trevor. Jonkanoo Village better wake up. (HIGH FIVES GIZZADA AND THEY DANCE TOGETHER) If is dance unno want fi dance, unno fi put down dat and learn di latest steps. Move wid me.
BENJAMIN:	Stop it. Dancers don't listen to Stagger Back. What does he know about dance?
STAGGER:	Is what do yuh Mas Benjy? Is me originate all di latest dance dem inna dis country. No say nutten.
BENJAMIN:	Well if you know so much bout dancing, why yuh don't join up wid di Jonkanoo band?
STAGGER:	Me is not a Jonkanoo. Dat a fi unno.
TREVOR:	Yow Stagger, just cool nuh man. Yuh cyah talk to di elder like dat.
BENJAMIN:	You stay dere laugh. Jonkanoo will come back and make this village proud again.
TREVOR:	Don't worry yuh self Mas Benjamin, dem just a talk uzimi.

BENJAMIN:	Me see you, but me nuh see dem. Ol' jagabatt dem. Don't know dem roots.
PRECIOUS :	You have all a wi support.
BENJAMIN:	I will fix this band and make it once more the Jonkanoo band of this island. Pitchy Patchy want some more liquid inna him waist, Devil some more fluid in you bones and Belly Woman you want more spirit in your body.
ZACKY:	What we need is a drink a whites Mas Benjamin. We can't dance Jonkanoo without waters fi wet di old bone dem. (SINGS) *We need more rum – fi play wha we play* *We need more rum – weh di rum bar deh* *We cyah throw leg without a half pint* *Rum just loosen up all wi joints* *We need more rum...*
BENJAMIN:	Stop it, no rum not drinking here til we have this year Jonkanoo parade ready.
BENJAMIN:	Listen to me. Over fifty years I making Jonkanoo in this village and not one holiday pass and we don't dance Jonkanoo for all the little pickney them and the whole town to enjoy. People come from far and wide to see our Jonkanoo celebrations every year. It is the main attraction and lifeblood of the town. If we kill it, we killing di town.
GIZZADA:	Well consider the town is dead. This is becoming a ghost town. All di duppy dem nuh want us here. (LAUGHS AND STAGGER BACK JOINS HER)

TREVOR: She has a point. Some of di people dem leaving one by one Mas Benjy. Dem fraid. Dem say Madda Lundi appear to dem and tell dem no more Jonkanoo must dance and we all must leave Jonkanoo village or bad tings going happen to people.

BENJAMIN: Dat is absolute rubbish. Madda Lundi is a good spirit and she like when we dance Jonkanoo.

PRECIOUS: Trevor, don't repeat such nonsense.

TREVOR: Mama, I just telling you what I hear people saying. Miss Rodina pack up her three youth and gone enuh mama.

GIZZADA: Yuh lie. A wha yuh a say to me?

TREVOR: Di people dem say is Madda Lundi beat down her door and say she fi leave Jonkanoo Village right away.

GIZZADA: Yuh lie. Well me nah stay here.

TREVOR: And other people leave too, saying di same thing.

PRECIOUS: Who else gone?

TREVOR: Missa Donovan. And the twin dem from round di back part a Jonkanoo village say dem a leave too.

GIZZADA: Yuh lie.

PRECIOUS: Gizzada!!! And is good riddance to those who want to go.

STAGGER: You see. Is all a dem superstitious duppy foolishness me cyah tek enuh. Its like Jonkanoo Village in di dark ages still.

PRECIOUS:	And dancehall is di light? You gwaan yuh ways yah. People, oonoo don't listen to all dat. Focus on what is at hand. You need more people fi join up di group Mass Benjamin. Dis too little.
VILLAGER:	We need more man. I will play di devil Mas Benjamin.
GIZZADA:	From me born me never see woman a play Jonkanoo. You would haffi be devil mumma. Woman don't business inna Jonkanoo business.
ZACKY:	Dats true, Jonkanoo is man thing. And we need more man.
GIZZADA:	Man shortage!
ADASA:	A true doh.
WOMEN:	*We need more man fi play wha wi play*
	We need more man. Whey di man dem deh?
	Di man dem nah step up to dem role
	A pure board man deh hol up light pole
	If dis community going get better
	Man and woman must join together
	Put di Jonkanoo back pon top
	Now di man dem a mek dancing flop
BENJAMIN:	*We need more strong man to play horse-head*
	We need Pitchy Patchy fi lead di parade
	Someone strong enough to play Ku Ku
GIZZADA:	*Yuh nah find dat inna di whole Jonkanoo*
	If you find one strong man inna di Village
	I want you send call me right away

No good man nah stay inna dis place

A pure walk foot man deh yah today

BENJAMIN: *We need a strong man to lead di parade*

Somebody strong who we all can trust

PRECIOUS: *Yes when di music play so sweet*

A man who can dance and lift up him feet

GIZZADA: *Me nuh why oonoo wasting time*

Tell me right now if a blind me blind

But if you find one strong man in di place

Him can lead my parade anytime

PRECIOUS: We're talking about dance.

GIZZADA: I'm talking about survival.

PRECIOUS: Jonkanoo is our survival.

GIZZADA: Yours not mine. What about you Trevor? Are you strong enough?

PRECIOUS: Him is not interested. Yes Mas Benjamin, we need to walk di village and select.

BENJAMIN: Di man dem not interested inna Jonkanoo again. All inna dem head is di boogoo-yagga dance what unno a jump up pon stage.

PRECIOUS: And it not getting them anywhere. But Trevor knows his roots. He will dance Jonkanoo.

TREVOR: Mama, why you always talking for me?

PRECIOUS: Because you not talking for yourself.

TREVOR: Mama.

PRECIOUS: What? Jonkanoo not good enough for you to dance anymore?

TREVOR: I never say dat. But I can talk for myself.

PRECIOUS:	So talk up, you not pickney nuh more.
STAGGER:	Trevor, tell dem say you is a dancehall man now nuh. A deh so di money deh enuh. Di dancer dem all a DJ now.
GIZZADA:	Yuh no hear say dancehall is export industry now mam? This year me alone export go a USA, Canada, Japan, England and farrin.
PRECIOUS:	Gizzada, Portmore is not farrin.
GIZZADA:	Close enough; Unno memba Bogle? Well ah me dem call Nanny.
STAGGER:	Just watch out fi di two a we pon Sumfest, East Fest, West Fest and Sting. Nuff more world tour and plenty stage show like dirt. Trevor, is better you come dance wid we and mek di money. Hey dat rhyme enuh. Mek me say dat again. Trevor come dance wid weee and mek di moneee? Oonoo like it?
ALL:	No.
STAGGER:	Me like it.
GIZZADA:	Me like it too yah Stagger and a money we say. Me no plan fi stay down yasso pon capture land for di rest of my life.
STAGGER:	Jonkanoo Village a dead stock now. So-so squatters.
PRECIOUS:	Squatters? Squatters? Watch yuh mouth Stagger Back. Is who yuh calling squatters? We are not squatters. We are legitimate informal settlers. We are just taking some time to formalize di papers for di informal part.
GIZZADA:	We no have no papers for Jonkanoo Village. Nutten cyah formalize here.

PRECIOUS:	We don't need papers fah down here in dis village. Miss Terrylonge has all of we papers.
GIZZADA:	So wheh she deh now? Miss Terrylonge deh a farrin. What a ting if when she comes back, she going to give di whole a we notice fi leave her property.
BENJAMIN:	She wouldn't do dat. That big house is the pride and glory of Jonkanoo Village. Every holiday Miss Terrylonge would a invite we up to her yard for party.
PRECIOUS:	And we would a dress up and look good inna we bashment clothes.
BENJAMIN:	And Mrs. Terrylonge would feed everybody and then officially start off the Jonkanoo parade. Then the band would start to play and we would dance, and dance.

THE VILLAGERS REMINISCE OF MISS TERRYLONGE'S PARTY AND THE JONKANOO BAND PLAYS ON AND THE DANCERS MOVE THE CROWD OFF STAGE.

BLACK-OUT

ACT I, SCENE 2

LATE AFTERNOON AT MR. BUCKINGSWORTH'S HOUSE. MR. BUCKINGWORTH AND MR. DONALDS, THE PARISH COUNCILLOR, MEET TO DISCUSS THEIR PLAN TO ACQUIRE THE JONKANOO VILLAGE PROPERTY OVER DINNER. THEIR WIVES ARE PRESENT.

MR. B:	Everything is going according to plan.
DONALDS:	Yes. Everything.
MR. B:	So Deal or No Deal? Come on Donald's say what's on your mind
DONALD'S	I'm gonna play my part.
MR.B:	How you gonna feel bout that.
DONALD'S:	Very Good.
	(SINGS)
	Deal or no Deal
MR.B:	(SINGS)
	I'm ready now to play the cards I've got
	I'm gonna get my share
	And that is how I feel bout that
	I will clear the place of all those squatters down there.
	Transform that jungle of Jonkanoo shacks with some quality care
	Jonkanoo Beach Village was once the pearl of Jamaica.
DONALDS:	(SINGS)
	I will help you make it so again, it's my duty as Parish Councilor.
	Is long overdue. And this is the plan

Somehow we have to get them off a di land.

I promised to develop the parish so here's the deal.

We keep it under wraps so there's no chance to appeal

At the next meeting of Parish Council I will approve your plans.

We spread a little money round so they hear our demands

If we play our cards right we get off squeaky clean

We can't appear to be doing harm to the low-life.

You know what I mean?

MRS. D: *I know exactly what you mean dear. (LAUGHS)*

So Deal or No Deal

It's not a question, it's a simple fact

They don't deserve this land

And that is how I feel bout that

MR. B: *I'm telling you Deal or no Deal*

It's time that we break down all those shacks

No need to be concerned

And that is how I feel bout that

DONALDS: I just don't want those human righters and environmentalists all over my back.

MRS. B: They are only doing what they think is best for the country, I suppose.

MR. B: Development is what's best for the country.

MRS. B: Yes but don't you think....

MR. B:	What I think is that Jonkanoo Beach Village must reclaim its glorious position as the most attractive tourist destination.
MRS. D:	Hear hear.
MRS. B:	That much I will agree with. So where you going to relocate the people?
MRS. D:	Relocate??? No Deal!!!
MR. B:	We going relocate dem out of the place.
DONALDS:	Look Mrs. B, for over thirty years dem wutliss Jonkanoos haven't paid one cent of property tax.
MRS. D:	They contribute nothing to the economy.
MRS. B:	I suppose you're right. But doesn't the property belong to Mrs. Terrylonge?
MR. B:	She should never have got that property when her husband died. I was in negotiations with the man to buy it. Look at how she left the place to these people.
MRS. B:	She went to give her husband the best care possible in the States, dear. That's all. Remember we all went to school together. When he died she just tried to make a living up there.
MR. B:	And leave the place to squatters?
MRS. D:	What a waste.
MRS. B:	She used to visit once a year.
MRS. D:	Well I haven't seen her in ages.
MRS. B:	Well, you still can't just claim her property.
MR. B:	(SINGS)
	Why not? That's what those squatters did.

> *At least I was honest and put in a bid*
>
> *But we are in a much better place*
>
> *I happen to know she's flat broke on her face.*
>
> *She paying back the medical bills with no saving grace.*
>
> *Her investments are gone*
>
> *That house and land is all she have left*
>
> *And she done mortgage it off to pay off all her debts,*
>
> *The hospital nearly sue her and lock up her parts*
>
> *So we have the upper hand and she don't have fart*

MRS. B: And you're going to try to take it away from her?

MR. B: Don't be so dramatic dear. I will purchase the property. I have the cash. She can't do anything with it anyway. She owes a ton of property taxes that she can't find any way to pay.

MRS. D: So you have her by the scruff off her neck. I must admit I never liked her in school. She always acted too big for her status.

MRS. B: She was a decent girl. With lots of ambition.

MRS. D: Well obviously ambition alone is not enough dear.

MR. B: *So Deal or No Deal*

> *It's not a question, it's a simple fact*
>
> *They don't deserve this land*
>
> *And that is how I feel bout that*

I'm telling you Deal or no Deal

It's time that we break down all those shacks

No need to be concerned

And that is how I feel bout that

MR. B: Enough of this talk Esmie. Mr. Donalds and I are talking business. You ladies can get back to the dinner party and we will be in shortly. Donalds how we stay? Seize di whole village and sell the property to the highest bidder. Plus I have other plans in the mix. I playing dem own card against dem. They are such a backward superstitious lot. This will be like taking candy from a baby.

DONALDS: First we need to issue a public notice of our intention to seize and wait thirty days, and then if the taxes are not paid up, it's all yours. But get them off. We don't want them in the mix when the deal goes down. But how you going to convince Miss Terrylonge?

MR. B: Miss Terrylonge is history. After she don't own nutten. She tek too long so just tell her dat it slip out of her hand. (HANDS DONALDS AN ENVELOPE) Dis is di deposit. Signed and seal. Deal?

DONALDS: Deal.

BLACK-OUT

Aston Cooke

ACT I, SCENE 3

SCENE MOVES FROM THE BUCKINGSWORTH TO A PATHWAY TO THE BEACH. PRECIOUS IS WALKING ALONE WITH BASKET OF FRESH FISH WHEN SHE HEARS A RUSTLING IN THE PATH BEHIND HER. SHE STOPS TO INVESTIGATE.

PRECIOUS:	Is who dat? Who dat a follow me? Me could a sure me hear somebody inna di bush back ah me. Trevor? Ah you dat? Mas Benjy? Who dat?
M LUNDI:	(VOICE IN THE DARK) Miss Precious. Miss Precious.
PRECIOUS:	Hello? Is who calling me name? What yuh want? Who is you?
M LUNDI:	Madda Lundi. Me name Madda Lundi.
PRECIOUS:	Madda Lundi? Look here, whoever is doing all a dis duppy foolishness you better cut it out. I don't' know what you selling but I not buying it. You hear me?
M LUNDI:	I am not a Duppy. I am Madda Lundi. I am not a legend. I am real.
PRECIOUS:	Duppy. The Lord is my Shepherd. I shall not want. Duppy. (SHE MARKS AND 'X' ON THE GROUND WITH A STICK) Get away Duppy, get away. Follow me if you tink you bad. (SHE MOVES AND SHE HEARS THE SOUND AGAIN) If you is real, mek mi see yuh face den. Stop hide and come out a di bush so show yuh face.
M LUNDI:	I am not hiding. Precious, I need your help.
PRECIOUS:	Me? What you want me to help you wid?

102

M LUNDI:	You must protect Jonkanoo Village and protect my resting place. I am your great, great, great, great, grand mother and my spirit is uneasy. These are my people. These are your people. Protect them. Protect the land.
PRECIOUS:	Protect dem from who? From what? Hello? Where you gone? Hello?
BENJAMIN:	(APPEARS) Miss Precious. What yuh doing out yah inna di night dew a chat to yuhself?
PRECIOUS:	Lord have mercy yuh nearly give me a heart attack. Mas Benjamin You see her?
BENJAMIN:	See who? Only you and I are here Precious.
PRECIOUS:	Madda Lundi.
BENJAMIN:	Look here. You are a sensible woman. I hope you are not believing all ah dem foolishness too. Somebody is up to mischief and I going to find out who it is.
BENJAMIN:	Me and Trevor doing some investigations.
PRECIOUS:	Yes Trevor. He is a bright young man dat yuh have enuh Precious. Di pride and joy of Jonkanoo village.
PRECIOUS:	I know but sometimes I think him too easily led astray.
BENJAMIN:	Just give him time. Him just finding himself. And he knows everybody. If anybody can help me get to the bottom of this duppy ting it's him. Somebody's up to no good.
PRECIOUS:	I agree with you but what happened to me was different. Is not as if somebody was trying to scare me. It felt real. Me was a gaze way little bit and go in a dream. Like a vision.
BENJAMIN:	What yuh vision Precious?

PRECIOUS:	Me see her. You ever see her yet Mas Benjy?
BENJAMIN:	See who? Who you really see?
PRECIOUS:	Madda Lundi, she was right here so. She talked to me. But she never showed her face.
BENJAMIN:	Madda Lundi? Madda Lundi nah show her face just so. Something would have to be very wrong for her to leave her world to come here. Madda Lundi is not happy, there is something brewing in Jonkanoo Village and it's not nice.

BLACK-OUT

ACT I, SCENE 4

A BUSY DAY ON JONKANOO BEACH AND THE EXTENT OF SQUATTING IS EVIDENT AS THE BEACH IS PESTERED WITH SHACKS AND THE INFAMOUS BLUE PLASTIC TENT-LIKE SHOPS WITH HIGGLERS SELLING ANYTHING FROM FISH AND FESTIVAL TO FRUITS. AS BATHERS ENTER, THE HIGGLERS APPROACH THEM EAGER TO MAKE A SALE. MISS PRECIOUS HAS THE LARGEST STALL (HUT) WITH HER SIGN "PRECIOUS FISH AND FESTIVAL". MRS. BUCKINGSWORTH, MRS. DONALDS AND YOUNG SARAH BUCKINGSWORTH ENTER.

VENDORS: (SING)

Fish, fish

Fish, fish, I'm cooking fish

Fish, fish, I'm selling fish

Fry fish, steam fish, or escoveitched

Di best fish come from Jonkanoo Beach

Follow we down to Jonkanoo Beach

Pretty sea water, mek sure yuh reach

We deh pon di beach all day long

Night and day we a sing dis song

Work and Play till night come dung

And we wait pon di morning sun

PRECIOUS: Come, come, unno move out of the way and make the nice, nice people dem come. Come dis way yuh hear ladies. They are my customers.

THE THREE LADIES MAKE THEIR WAY TO PRECIOUS' STALL AND SPREAD THEIR TOWELS ON A MAKE-SHIFT WODDEN BEACH CHAIR.

MRS. D:	LOUD WHISPER. Mrs. Buckingsworth dear, I don't know why we have to come down to his place.
MRS. B:	Because here is where you'll get the best fish and bammy and festival on the island.
MRS. D:	I hope they'll wash their hands. I don't see any running water and they fry the fish on a coal stove with open flames.
MRS. B:	Culture dear, its called culture. Every now and then we have to stoop and enjoy the culture of the masses.
MRS. D:	Mr. Donalds should come down here and just level all these shacks. The beach would be much more pleasant for all to enjoy.
MRS. B:	Icy, it is good for us to see how they live.
MRS. D:	See me and live wid me are two different things my dear.
PRECIOUS:	Excuse me. Good day Mrs. Buckingsworth and Mrs. Donalds. What unno want today ladies? What can get I fah unno?
VENDORS:	(SINGS)

Fish, fish

Fish, fish, I'm cooking fish

Fish, fish, I'm selling fish

Fry fish, steam fish, or escoveitched

Di best fish come from Jonkanoo Beach

Jack fish, parrot, sprat and snapper

Escallion, thyme, scotch bonnet pepper

Carrot, cho-cho, ockro and little butter

Taste dis fish and lick off you finger |

> *Peppered shrimp, crab and lobster*
>
> *Cooked to order, anyway you prefer*
>
> *Wash it down wid coconut water*
>
> *Den go swim inna de sea water*

SARAH: I want fried lobster with festival

MRS. B: Precious dear, you know I want one of the big hog snapper with bammy. And Precious dear, bring a small steamed fish for Mrs. Donalds and Precious, do some extra bammies and festivals.

PRECIOUS: At your service mam. Your fried fish are coming up right away.

MRS. B: What you have to drink?

PRECIOUS: Trevor, Trevor. Trevor's coming ma'am. Me son, Trevor will help unno at the bar.

TREVOR: Yes mamma.

PRECIOUS: Trevor, look after the ladies with drinks. (TREVOR ENTERS)

SARAH: Hi Trevor. (APPROACHES THE BAR) Hi. What you have to cool me down?

TREVOR: What you want? You know you can have anything you want, from the bar.

SARAH: Then what you think ah talking about? You have any bottled water?

TREVOR: (HE SERVES) See them here. Mamma, collect for three water.

SARAH: Thanks Trevor. Oh Trevor, we want you to join Quadrille Heights group for the big dance competition this year.

TREVOR:	You mad? What would mamma and the rest of Jonkanoo Village think if I was to represent Quadrille Heights.
SARAH:	It's up to you. Think about it and let me know.

JOYCE ENTERS AND WITNESSES SOMETHING GOING ON BETWEEN TREVOR AND SARAH. SHE SNAPS AT THEM AS SARAH MAKES HER WAY AWAY FROM THE BAR.

JOYCE:	Think about nutten. Gwaan to yuh mumma.
PRECIOUS:	Shhh, why yuh doan leave yuh coarseness at yuh doorstep? Nuh come ah road wid it.
JOYCE:	Yuh no see di little ripe pickney a put question to Trevor behind yuh back?
PRECIOUS:	Is young people dem name. And furthermore, Trevor and her went to school together, she means no harm.
JOYCE:	Quadrille Heights fi look dem one another up a Quadrille Heights and leave Jonkanoo people dem alone. Dem come a Jonkanoo beach fi yam fish, dem not to come here to catch shark.
PRECIOUS:	We haffi just put up wid dem till we collect di money. Trevor. You all right?
TREVOR:	Me cool Mamma, me can take care of myself. She's only suggest dat me dance inna dem group for the competition.
JOYCE:	See it there Miss Precious. Now she wants Trevor to dance fah Quadrille Heights. Trevor is not a Quadrille dancer, he has Jonkanoo inna him blood.
PRECIOUS:	I hope yuh told her no. Come, the fish dem ready. Joyce, help me serve this.

PRECIOUS AND JOYCE TAKE THE FOOD TO THE LADIES.

ZACKY:	(ENTERS) Boat come in, fish come Miss Precious. I bring some of the best snapper and doctor fish for you.
PRECIOUS:	Thanks Mas Zacky. Trevor, I want you take some of this fish up to Mas Benjamin. He is at Mrs. Terrylonge's house.
ZACKY:	Is fish like this Miss Terrylonge would a love herself?
PRECIOUS:	You know if she never deh a farrin, I would a fry some and tek it up there myself.

TREVOR ASSISTS ZACKY WITH THE UNLOADING OF THE FISH AND BOTH EXIT WITH THE EMPTY CONTAINERS TOWARDS THE BOATS.

JOYCE:	Miss Precious, anybody hear from Miss Terrylonge a farrin?
PRECIOUS:	Mouth say she a come back a Jonkanoo Village.
JOYCE:	Is fine time she come back. Cause I don't know what she is doing wid di big house down here and she is all the way ah farrin?
PRECIOUS:	Dat is none of our business Joyce. Ask her when she comes.
JOYCE:	Den she a come before next holiday? If not, we could a open it up for this holiday and have a big bashment party.
PRECIOUS:	You must be mad.
JOYCE:	Me no mad mam. Look how many years since she fenced the nice property and gone a farrin. Let us use it and keep a big Passa Passa. Charge to come in and raise money to buy new Jonkanoo costume for Mas Benjy and di man dem.
PRECIOUS:	Miss Terrylonge left Mas Benjy as caretaker of the house.

MRS. BUCKINGSWORTH, SARAH AND MRS. DONALDS ARE FINISHED WITH THEIR MEALS. THEY PACK UP AND PREPARE TO LEAVE.

PRECIOUS:	(TO HER CUSTOMERS) You all done? How was it?
MRS. B:	Good as always. I always enjoy your fried fish Precious dear. We will back another time.
MRS. D:	(UNDER HER BREATH) By that time it would have been transformed to a much more decent and customer friendly environment.
PRECIOUS:	What did you say Mrs. D?
MRS. B:	(POKES MRS. D) She says, your fried fish is very environmentally delicious that you are friendly to the customers.
PRECIOUS:	Oh thank you very much mam. Everybody always tell me dat. When visitor come a wi fireside, we mek we pot smell sweet.
SARAH:	Trevor? Where is Trevor Miss Precious?
PRECIOUS:	Him gone a sea with Mas Zacky.
JOYCE:	Harbour shark is out deh yuh fi go after him. Yuh look like a mermaid and an octopus.
SARAH:	Tell him bye for me.
JOYCE:	Him say bye to you too. Pickney, yuh don't understand English? Well understand dis, me say, yuh fi tek way yuh self from bout yah.

THE LADIES EXIT. JOYCE AND PRECIOUS WAVE. AS THEY LEAVE, TREVOR RUSHES IN.

TREVOR:	Mamma, mamma, Corporal Clappers a look for you.
PRECIOUS:	What him want? After mi no criminal. What police a look for me fah?

SHADOW: (CLAPPERS AND SHADOW ENTER) Miss Precious Adamson. Calling Miss Precious Adamson.

PRECIOUS: Dat is me name. What is di matter?

JOYCE: And as usual his shadow is behind him.

SHADOW: Watch yuh mouth woman. Mind me arrest you.

JOYCE: Arrest me fi what Shadow? I didn't address you sar, I was speaking to Miss Precious.

PRECIOUS: What is di problem Officer? We no need no police pon di beach. We are safe down here.

JOYCE: Attention Corporal Clappers is here.

CLAPPERS: I am an emissary from Mr. Alexander Buckingsworth, and he has sent me with a message for your attention. ASP Clappers at your service.

JOYCE: Did you get a promotion from di commissioner? Since when yuh turn ASP?

PRECIOUS: What is the message Corporal Clappers?

CLAPPERS: I need to see you in camera.

PRECIOUS: Me no inna no camera business wid police Clappers. Anything you want to say to me yuh better say it in front of everybody. Tek di picture in public.

CLAPPERS: Do you have the authority to speak on behalf of the rest of the people?

PRECIOUS: But of course, I am the President of the Jonkanoo Village Informal Settler Association. I represent all of di people dem down here pon di beach.

VILLAGERS: True. Talk to Miss Precious. Is she yuh fi talk to. She represents di whole a we. A we agent dat.

CLAPPERS: Well I was instructed to read it aloud and personally deliver this notice to you all.

SHADOW: In the presence of two witnesses.

PRECIOUS: Nuff witnesses pon di beach. Hurry up and read. Yuh can read? What it say?

CLAPPERS: (READS) *"Notice is hereby served to all squatters on that parcel of land, Volume 9999, Folio 2222, known as Jonkanoo Village, to vacate said property in thirty days."*

SHADOW: Yes, thirty days. *"Failure to do so will result in forceful eviction. The owner will not accept liability for any erection, material or property damaged or removed in the clearing of the said property. Signed, Property Owner."*

JOYCE: And who is di property owner? Who sent you to us Clappers?

CLAPPERS: You may address all further correspondences and dat mean questions and queries to Mr. Buckingsworth who sign him name pon top of the space where it say property owner. See it here. (HANDS PRECIOUS THE NOTICE) See him sign deh.

SHADOW AND CLAPPERS LEAVE AS THE CROWD BECOMES HOSTILE AND HURL STONES AND THEM.

VILLAGERS: Evict who? Go away, Move. Nobody can put we off a dis land. Tell Mr. Buckingsworth fo go way. Nutten cyan go so. Bacra massa time done now. Him cyan dweet.

BLACK-OUT

ACT I, SCENE 5

MAS BENJAMIN'S HOUSE. THE CITIZENS OF JONKANOO VILLAGE GATHER FOR A MEETING IN MAS BENJAMIN'S JONKANOO COSTUME WORKSHOP.

PRECIOUS: My fellow citizens of Jonkanoo....

As I stand here before oonoo

It's time for us to make a decision

Time to stand as one....

But before we begin our procession

We ask di lord's intervention

Sister Adasa will pray for us

ADASA: Dear Lord, come down and bless dis meeting. For the enemies come like pestilence to drive us away from di land. Protect us against all wicked and evil people, crosses and tribulations.

PRECIOUS: Dis meeting is short notice. But there is eminent threat against our abode. Mouth say dat Mr. Buckingsworth is planning to evict us from our home. We know that if we allow him to win it would be a sin, because the truth is that this property, doesn't belong to him.

PRECIOUS: Dem a call we hustlers

VILLAGERS: Who dem a chat?

PRECIOUS: Dem a call we parasites

VILLAGERS: Tek dat back!

PRECIOUS: Dem a call we squatters

VILLAGERS: We no name dat!

PRECIOUS:	All dem want to do is take what we got. We are informal settlers
VILLAGERS:	Yes - Informal settlers
CLAPPERS:	But even with all a dat oonoo still have to come off di people dem property. According to the Section 24 of the Property Law of Jamaica, di land don't belong to none of unno either.
PRECIOUS:	What are you doing here? Who invite you here?
CLAPPERS:	I live in Jonkanoo Village too. Shadow and I are police, and so dat means I can go anywhere in dis jurisdiction dat I want to go.
JOYCE:	Go back where unno coming from. And carry yuh ugly shadow too.
CLAPPERS:	Watch yuh mouth when addressing an officer. You are obstructoning the government's work.
PRECIOUS:	All right Corporal Clappers, you can stay, but make sure yuh carry di message correct. Tell Mr. Buckingsworth say dat we say dat none a we nah move from yasso.
CLAPPERS:	After me not a news carrier mam, me is a police. A.S.P. Clappers.
PRECIOUS:	A.S.P. or A.S.S. please tell Mr. Buckingsworth say him nuh have no authority fi put we off a Mrs. Terrylonge property? So hear what we saying to you...
VILLAGERS:	(SING)
	We not going no where
	We staying right here
	We nah move an inch

Though we feeling di pinch

It seems like the whole world

Just deh pon wi case

But we nah move

We nah move - not leaving dis place

Dem say a capture we capture de land

Say, we no pay dem money for lease

Well its time di whole a we take a stand

No land, no justice, and no peace

So we not going no where

We staying right here

We nah move an inch

Tho we feeling di pinch

It seems like the whole world

Just deh pon wi case

But we nah move

We nah move - not leaving dis place

CLAPPERS:	Well is long time Mrs. Terrylonge missing in action. Di land up for grabs cause Mrs. Terrylonge lost. All dis long talking is not a transaction
PRECIOUS:	So tell me since Buckingsworth a your boss
CLAPPERS:	(SINGS)
	My boss is the law and facts is fact

Oonoo don't have no papers

And dat is dat

If you have a plan you better prepare

Take the notice you get and beware

If you know what I know you pack up and gwaan

PRECIOUS: You don't have no heart, you're just Buckingsworth pawn

VILLAGERS: (SING)

But we not going no where

We staying right here

We nah move an inch

Tho we feeling di pinch

It seems like the whole world

Just deh pon wi case

But we nah move

We nah move - not leaving dis place

ZACKY: So him plan fi lock down the fishing village?

PRECIOUS: Him want to clear down di whole a we off a di land what we live pon.

ADASA: Well to tell the truth, none a we don't have nutten to show dat it rightfully belongs to us.

BENJAMIN: Neither does he. Make Mr. Buckingsworth produce papers wid signature pon it fi show dat him own the land. Mrs. Terrylonge never sold it to him. Her husband left it to her when he died.

PRECIOUS: Mr. Buckingsworth a use him head pon we. If we ketch we fraid and move, him just take it over without any trouble.

ADASA: I didn't lease anywhere from him. Is not him me paying me money to.

BENJAMIN: Sister Adasa, there is no lease on the house you live inna.

ADASA: Is Massa God land. See my landlord up deh. (POINTS UP) Only him can come down here now and give me notice from him land. Glory.

BENJAMIN: Well the notice dem send seems legal. Dem say Miss Terrylonge owes di government plenty money.

ADASA: How much? Make we drop church collection and pay.

PRECIOUS: Plenty money Sister Adasa. Trevor have the information pon di property. Him study it all night, he can explain it.

JOYCE: Trevor, come this side. Trevor, come here and explain it you hear.

GIZZADA: Why all the man dem in Jonkanoo Village not bright like Trevor?

PRECIOUS: Gizzada listen, mind me put you out of the meeting. Yuh tink is joke business this? Trevor talk you hear.

TREVOR: Everybody live here long time. But no one ever tried fi regularize dem status pon de land.

ZACKY: We no need fi regularized nutten. Miss Terrylonge say we could stay as long as we want. She never did mind.

TREVOR:	Well plenty money is owed to the government. Dem going to dispose of the land by selling it to Mr. Buckingsworth to get di money.
JOYCE:	Miss Terrylonge no owe Mr. Buckingsworth no money. Nutten no go so.
PRECIOUS:	Trevor never say dat Joyce. Deaf ears give liars trouble. Is tax money she owes to di government.
JOYCE:	Which one of di tax? I never know you pay GCT pon land too? Is plenty money?
TREVOR:	One million dollars.
CLAPPERS:	One million. Where unno squatters fi get dat breed a money to pay?
PRECIOUS:	Watch yuh mouth Clappers. Who you calling squatter Corporal Clappers? We are not squatters, we are legitimate Informal Settlers.
VILLAGERS:	Yes, we not squatters. True Miss Precious. Who yuh a call so? Not a squatter. We are informal settlers.
CLAPPERS:	Yes, I know...Informal meaning No Papers – Settlers meaning Squatters. Come off di property. This is your final warning.
ADASA:	The Lord will prepare a place in heaven for his children.
CLAPPERS:	You better tell him dat unno need somewhere right now pon earth.
ADASA:	Corporal Clappers and Shadow. I think dat unno have overstayed unno welcome.
CLAPPERS:	Come Shadow, mek we gwaan, we have police work to do.

PRECIOUS:	(TO POLICE AS THEY LEAVE) Trouble deh a bush, anancy carry come a yard. Remember to deliver the message to Mr. B. Tell him dat we nah go anywhere.
TREVOR:	Mamma, Mr. Buckingsworth is only taking advantage of a clumsy situation with the government.
PRECIOUS:	So Trevor, how much time we have to come up with this tax money?
TREVOR:	Thirty days. By end of the month, or else we must vacate or be evicted.
BENJAMIN:	We must be here to celebrate and dance Jonkanoo in the village for the holiday a come. Di people looking forward to it.
TREVOR:	Jonkanoo is what get we in this state. We can't go on dancing this Jonkanoo thing all day and night.
PRECIOUS:	Is which side yuh deh pon Trevor? Member say yuh is a born Jonkanoo.
TREVOR:	I know I am a Jonkanoo, but I don't have to live like Jonkanoo. We need to get with the times. We must try and earn some money for ourselves, which we can use to pay off the tax for Miss Terrylonge.
JOYCE:	Let's put on a big dance inna di square and charge di people to come in.
GIZZADA:	We sell tickets and sell tings like curry goat and drinks. Miss P, you could fry some fish and contribute.
BENJAMIN:	I will do anything to save we Jonkanoo and save we village. For if we don't save Jonkanoo, Madda Lundi will not forgive us.

JOYCE:	You come back with that fool-fool Madda Lundi thing again Mas Benjy. That is what is terrifying the people mek nuff a dem run away.
BENJAMIN:	Dat is not Madda Lundi. But we on di case.
PRECIOUS:	She a watch and protect dis village.
TREVOR:	All right Mas Benjamin, Let us do it for Madda Lundi's sake. Let us organize the biggest street dance dat Jonkanoo Village ever see and raise dat one million dollars. Agreed?
VILLAGERS:	Yes, Yes. We agree. True. Agree.

(SING)

But we not going no where

We staying right here

We nah move an inch

Tho we feeling di pinch

It seems like the whole world

Just deh pon wi case

But we nah move

We nah move - not leaving dis place

BLACK-OUT

ACT I, SCENE 6

VILLAGE SQUARE. BUCKINGSWORTH ALONG WITH HIS SURVEYING TEAM OF CLAPPERS, DONALDS AND SHADOW ARE MARKING ON THE LAND AND DISCUSSING THE DESIGN AND CONSTRUCTION OF THE NEW HOTEL.

MR.B:	Stretch the marker more to the right. I will build the hotel over here and as soon as I knock down these shacks I will put the golf course over there.
JOYCE:	Knock down where so sar? Is who fah abode you a call shack sah?
CLAPPERS:	Miss Joyce, move out of di way and make di decent man do him work.
JOYCE:	Yuh is a traitor Clappers. Yuh is a sell-out.
CLAPPERS:	What yuh talking about? You have your work and I have my work.
JOYCE:	But a lef yuh to Miss Terrylonge when she comes.
DONALDS:	When she comes? Mr. Buckingsworth, don't listen to them, they are only trying to scare you off the land.
MR. B:	Clappers what are they talking about?
CLAPPERS:	Well sar, me only did hear a little ting. And I don't fully investigate it as yet.
MR. B:	What is it that you heard?
CLAPPERS:	Me hear dat Mrs. Terrylonge send a telegram pon di Internet, via email, inna di computer say dat she coming soon to deal wid matters.
JOYCE:	Dat is correct. She ah come fah true.

MR. B: Too late, too late. Let her come. I have a trump card in my back pocket.

DONALDS: What we going to do?

MR. B: We will speed up the eviction and get them off before dat troublemaker woman come. She is always trying to put a spoke in everything that I do. She thinks she is 'bull buck and duppy conqueror' everywhere she go. Well I am going cramp her style this time. Let her come.

BLACK-OUT

ACT I, SCENE 7

BUCKINGSWORTH'S VERANDAH. THE BUCKINGSWORTHS MEET
WITH THE PARISH COUNCILLOR AND HIS WIFE FOR AFTERNOON
TEA. ADASA IS THEIR HIRED HELP IN THE HOUSE.

MRS. B: Adasa, Adasa.

ADASA: (ENTERS) Yes mam. Dassa me name mam. What is it please mam?

MRS. B: How comes yuh didn't tell me dat our dear friend is returning to Jonkanoo Village?

ADASA: Who ma'am? I don't fast inna odda people business. I doan know what you talking bout.

MRS. D: She's talking about your village queen Miss Terrylonge. Esmie, these hired help always play dumb when it suits them.

ADASA: Excuse me ma'am?

MRS. D: You're excused. Run along. Bring out a pot of tea for us.

ADASA: I don't work for you enuh ma'am. And I don't run along for you nor nobody.

MRS. D: Excuse me.

ADASA: You're excused. Would you like some tea Mrs. B?

MRS. B: Yes Adasa. Thank you. (ADASA LEAVES)

MRS. D: You give that girl far too much leeway. She is out of order.

MRS B: So Terrylonge coming back after all. I Haven't seen her in a while.

MRS.D: Her presence is neither here nor there. It's just a matter of time. Soon dat little Jonkanoo Village will be history.

MRS. B:	But they have no intention to leave the land. They will put up a fight. I think we disregard them at our own peril.
MRS. D:	Fight for what? They better leave it or else.
DONALDS:	(ENTERS) They're holding on to something down there. I sent two trucks to do the work and the truck drivers said, they are afraid to go down there.
MRS. D:	We can't let these Jonkanoo hooligans win.
DONALDS:	They're a stubborn set of people. But they are running scared now. Lots of talk about duppies and spirits. People leaving one by one.
MRS. B:	How convenient. What is that all about?
DONALDS:	I have no idea. But it's all good. They need to go. They don't own a piece of land down there.
MRS. D:	I'm sure it's the old man Mas Benjy leading them. I must admit I never liked him. I suspect Mas Benjamin is dem obeah man.

ADASA RETURNS WITH A TRAY OF TEA POT AND CUPS AND SAUCERS. SHE BUTTS IN THE CONVERSATION.

ADASA:	Mas Benjy is not a obeah man. And Madda Lundi is not a duppy.
MRS. D:	Madda Lundi or Madda Terrylonge, none of them has rights to this land.
MR. B:	(ENTERS) They're going to need more than duppies and obeah to pay off the one million dollars back-tax on the land.
DONALDS:	Jonkanoo Beach will soon be yours.
MRS. B:	We will certainly miss the little ethnic Jonkanoo culture thing they do.

MRS. D:	Culture? Jumping up and down like idiots dressed in rags? What part of that is culture? The Quadrille Heights dancers show them a thing or two about culture when we win the National Dance Competition.
MRS. B:	This much we can agree on. But we need another male dancer. I noticed Sarah shining up to that nice young man Trevor.
ALL:	What?
MR. B:	I don't want him around my daughter. And we don't need him. By the hook or by the crook we will win and teach those Jonkanoos a lesson once and for all.

ADASA EDGES CLOSE TO THE CONVERSATION, SHE LISTENS.

ADASA:	Don't be so sure sar. Jonkanoo people dem can dance better than unno up here a Quadrille Heights. And dis part a di country is Jonkanoo country so no other dance cyah beat we.
MR. B:	Adasa. Who is talking to you? You pass your place again?
ADASA:	No sar. Me just ah talk to myself sar.
MR. B:	Clear up now. Hurry up and go home to your Jonkanoo Village.
ADASA:	Are you finished with me Mrs. B?
MRS. B:	Yes Adasa you may go. (ADASA EXITS)
MR. B:	How dare you. Esmie, I tell you I don't like that, that, that...gyal. She's damn out of order.
MRS. B:	Perhaps if you weren't so rude to her she wouldn't be so rude to you in return dear. She has feelings.

MR. B:	She is a low-life, class-less, gutter-snipe. I don't care about her feelings.
MRS. B:	And I'm sure she realizes that…dear.
MR. B:	Look, I am not having this argument with you again…in front of our guests. I don't understand why you defend those people. You're born with a gold spoon in your mouth, so don't pretend you understand their Jonkanoo ways.
MRS. B:	I am Jamaican, I love my culture and all of it is my culture.
MR. B:	Your culture is here, with us in Quadrille Heights. Quadrille Heights will win the dance competition. No duppies or spirits can stop my plan. We will win. I will see to it.

BLACK-OUT

ACT I, SCENE 8

JONKANOO VILLAGE SQAURE. IT IS LATE SATURDAY NIGHT AND THE VILLAGERS MOUNT A VIGIL IN THE SQUARE. VILLAGERS HOLD HANDS ACROSS THE MAIN STREET OF THE VILLAGE SQUARE. THERE IS SOME TENSION AS THEY AWAIT AN EVICTION. THE VILLAGERS LIGHT CANDLES.

PRECIOUS: How we stay? Stagger Back, are we ready for di eviction?

STAGGER: Everything is everything Miss Precious.

PRECIOUS: Gizzada, are you all right?

GIZZADA: Everything turn on. Nutten no plug out, everything plug een.

BENJAMIN: Why this likkle girl don't speak decent patois dat me can understand. Who nuh plug in? Who turn on? What yuh mean?

JOYCE: We ready for dem Miss Precious. Not even di army could ah pass through this human barricade today. But oonoo sure dem coming before di time even up?

ADASA: Mr. Buckingsworth say him a come today. Me hear dem a whisper in di house all week. They want to catch us off guard. They said Mr. Buckingsworth is sending a bulldozer and crane down yasso to scrape up di whole a we down here in Jonkanoo Village.

PRECIOUS: Scrape up who? After we no hog and goat? Make dem come.

BENJAMIN: Yes, we ready for him. And none ah dem can't cross dis barrier.

VILLAGERS: (SING)

Can't cross the barrier – the barrier

Right here and now is the line that we draw

Mek dem know- we serious

And nobody knows what will happen

If they ever stand before us

Poor people try our best to get ahead but we can't

We have a right to live in homes

Like everybody else that's why

They can't cross the barrier – the barrier

TREVOR: You know what I don't understand? Why dem don't just invest in the Jonkanoo festival we have every year. Look how many people it draw from near and far.

BENJAMIN: Dem shortsighted bout culture man. They think its only sand and beach which draw tourist to Jamaica. Its di culture and di energy that people want to feel why dem come. But cow nuh know di use a him tail till him lose it. And is war down here tonight. If him tink him bad, make him come.

TREVOR: No Mas Benjamin, no war going fight around here.

ADASA: That's right. This is peaceful protest Mas Benjamin. Remember we are Christian soldiers.

PRECIOUS: True Sister Adasa, after we not war-boat. We Jonkanoo people is God fearing and loving people. But what we must do when dem come.

ADASA: We have the Lord on our side Miss Precious. The creator owns this land.

BENJAMIN: The law is not on our side Sister Adasa.

ADASA:	Jesus is on our side. We don't need anyone else. We are covered in the blood. *"When the wicked, even mine enemies and my foes came upon me to eat up my flesh, they stumbled and fell."* Glory.
TREVOR:	Just be calm all of you. We just have to handle it properly and don't allow this to get out of hand.
PRECIOUS:	Trevor, we are all right. We are all right. We are not giving trouble, we just ah guard the place as you say we must do.

THERE IS MUCH EXCITEMENT AS LOUD CAR HORN BLARES AND DRAWS THEIR ATTENTION. A LARGE AIRPORT TAXI (MINI BUS) PULLS UP IN THE SQUARE AND THE CROWD GATHERS. MISS TERRYLONGE ALIGHTS FROM THE TAXI

FOLLOWED BY MALIKA.

VILLAGERS:	She come. Miss Terrylonge come back. See her deh. She look good.
BENJAMIN:	Welcome back home Miss Terrylonge.
PRECIOUS:	Miss Terrylonge we glad yuh come home fi true true true.
MISS T:	Oh thanks. Mas Benjy, yuh don't age one bit. Miss Precious, is that you?
PRECIOUS:	Is me same one Miss T.
MISS T:	Precious, you no stop wear those short skirts? Yuh not young again you know.
PRECIOUS:	Miss T, you know it shows my youthful figure and dat is all I have left right now.
MISS T:	Larks, you all keep yourselves looking good. You ah go mek water come from me eye.
PRECIOUS:	(ACKNOWLEDGING MALIKA) And who is dis mam? Is this your daughter mam?
BENJAMIN:	Daughter? Precious don't be forward.

MISS T:	(BRINGS MALIKA FORWARD) See her here, dis is Malika, mi first grand daughter. She born ah farrin.
BENJAMIN:	Pleased to meet you Miss Malika.
PRECIOUS:	Your name very pretty like you.
MALIKA:	Thanks very much. I am just happy to be here with grandma. Good to meet you all.
PRECIOUS:	We are all family. Miss Terrylonge is always good to us. She is mother to everyone in Jonkanoo Village.
BENJAMIN:	She is like Jonkanoo mumma.
MISS T:	But look at this. You all turn up here to greet my arrival. This is so heart-warming. How oonoo know I was coming?
GIZZADA:	(LOOKING OUT) Dem ah come. Dem ah come.
MISS T:	Who ah come? What is happening?
GIZZADA:	Corporal Clappers and Shadow a lead dem come down the beach.
TREVOR:	We need to get you inside the house ma'am and I will help Miss Malika with her bags.
PRECIOUS:	Dis is Trevor ma'am. My big son.

TREVOR FLIRTS WITH MALIKA AS HE HELPS HER WITH HER BAGS.

TREVOR:	Yes, I am Trevor at your service. Come this way madam.
MALIKA:	Thank you sir.
MISS T:	A lady's gentleman. Larks, him grow nice fi true.
TREVOR:	I will escort you with your accommodation, quickly before…
MISS T:	Before what? What is going on?

BUCKINGSWORTH, CORPORAL CLAPPERS AND SHADOW ENTER AHEAD OF A CRANE AND TRACTOR. THERE IS MUCH NOISE AND COMMOTION AS THE TRACTOR AND THE CRANE PULL UP TO THE SITE. WORKMEN TAKE UP POSITION IN FRONTOF THE MACHINES.

VILLAGERS:	(SING)
	Can't cross the barrier – the barrier
	Right here and now is the line that we draw
	Mek dem know- we serious
	And nobody knows what will happen
	If they ever stand before us
	Poor people try our best to get ahead but we can't
	We have a right to live in homes
	Like everybody else that's why
	They can't cross the barrier – the barrier
MISS T:	But ah no Clappers dat? Come here Clappers. Carry me bag for me.
CLAPPERS:	Who goes?
MISS T:	Who goes where? Shet yuh mouth and tek up me bag dem Clappers.
CLAPPERS:	Oh it's you Miss Terrylonge? What are you doing here? Yuh get visa to enter di country?
MISS T:	I don't need visa fi come a Jonkanoo. I live here. I come as I like. Stop di talking and help mi carry di bags dem up to di house.
CLAPPERS:	Me is not yard boy anymore mam. Me is police now. A.S.P. Clappers.

MISS T:	You could be Governor General or Commissioner of Police. Just help me carry me bag dem.
PRECIOUS:	Anybody tell you yet mam? Mas Benjy, you no tell Miss T yet?
MISS T:	Tell me what? Benjamin, what unno hiding from me?
BENJAMIN:	Miss T, we did want you to settle down first before we bother you wid we troubles.
MISS T:	Me settle from di plane land Mas B. Jonkanoo Village trouble is my trouble. What is it that I should know that I don't know?
PRECIOUS:	Notice. We got notice fi come off ah di land mam.
MISS T:	Notice? But nobody can't give unno dat? Which part it di notice come from?
PRECIOUS:	Mr. Buckingsworth mam. He sent Corporal Clappers and Shadow down yah to we wid di eviction notice.
MISS T:	Me is di only smaddy who could do dat, and I didn't issue nothing of the sort.
PRECIOUS:	Between him and Mr. Donalds, dem say you owe million dollars fi tax so dem is reclaiming di land.
BENJAMIN:	Well I believe we can raise the money and pay for it. Dats why we never tink it necessary to bother you a farrin.
MISS T:	Dat anancy man Mr. Buckingsworth is more than forward. Is who fah land him romping wid? Him love red-eye what no belong to him. I will deal wid him.
CLAPPERS:	In the name of the law, unno move!

THE VILLAGERS DRAW CLOSER TOGETHER AND THEY PREPARE
TO DEFEND THEIR PROPERTY.

PRECIOUS:	Eviction. Evict who? Backra massa time done long time now. Go tell Mr. Buckingsworth say dat him going haffi use di crane to lift me up. Is who yuh ah evict?
GIZZADA:	Shadow. Shadow. Unno cyaan touch mi tings dem. Corporal Clappers, gwaan back a Quadrille Heights.
SHADOW:	Unno obstructing the work of the law.
GIZZADA:	Gway from me Shadow, you is just a duppy shadow for Mr. Buckingsworth.
PRECIOUS:	Why you don't send him come personally?
SHADOW:	Mr. Buckingsworth say all you squatters fi come off him property tonight, tonight.
MR.B:	STEPPING FORWARD. Squatters, settler, whatever unno call it. All a unno fi go back inna di hole where unno come from.
PRECIOUS:	Clear off Mr. Buckingsworth. After nobody no come from inna hole more dan you. Gway.
TREVOR:	Watch yuh self enuh big man. Watch yuh self.
CROWD:	Mek him Gway. Move from yah. A how him so bad?
GIZZADA:	Trevor strong eeh.
BENJAMIN:	No bother wid him Trevor. As you say before don't start nutten, we don't want no confrontation.
MR.B:	Unno want confrontation and unno no live no where. If unno refuse fi move off di land, well I have given instructions to push unno off.

THE CROWD PARTS TO GIVE MISS TERRYLONGE WAY TO CENTRE
STAGE. SHE WAVES THE TITLE IN HAND.

MISS T:	(ENTERING) And who gives you that authority fi carry out this illegal eviction?
MR. B:	Who dat? You are all in violation of the law. Look from when unno get notice to vacate?
MISS T:	Notice from who? I, Hyacinth Terrylonge is the rightful and legal proprietor of this piece of land known as Jonkanoo Village.
CLAPPERS:	Proprietor which part? Mr. Buckingsworth say dat unno is all here illegally.
MISS T:	Clappers move out a me way.
CLAPPERS:	A.S.P. Clappers. Address me properly when you addressing me.
MISS T:	Suck-finger Clappers. Dat is di name yuh mother give to you when you was little and wouldn't stop suck yuh finger. You stop it yet? Move.
CLAPPERS:	Aahm...well...ahm...Yes ma'am.
MR.B:	Listen to me, Miss Terrylonge. Everyone in this village seems to have respect for you. They listen to you. Why you just don't tell them to vacate the property and allow for a smooth development of the property. Or else I will demolish dem myself.
MISS T:	If you touch one thing, you will be the one getting demolished tonight. Here is the title for the property. And nowhere on it I see the name Buckingsworth.
PRECIOUS:	Take dat Mr. Buckingsworth. Mawga cow a bull mumma.
MR.B:	Title, that is of no use now. You are one million dollars in arrears for property tax. Which part unno can find dat by end of month? So move with your bogus title.

MISS T:	Bogus nutten. (SHE READS) Listen to it for yourself. *"Certificate of Title under the Registration of Titles Act. Miss Hyacinth Terrylonge, is the proprietor of that parcel of land known as Jonkanoo Beach Village. Signed Registrar of Titles."*
MR. B:	(SPEAKS SOFTLY TO MISS T) You and I both know that title is not worth the paper it's written on. I know how much in debt you are for this house and I'm not just talking about the property tax. You know what I mean.
MISS T:	Why you and Mr. Donalds so sneaky? Yuh hide yuh stick and lick di people. Unno can tek unno notice and roll it up and nyam it. I want you and yuh demolition team to leave right away, this is private property. Don't let me call the superintendent of Police to handle the case.
MR. B:	We will go for now. But I suggest you call up your creditors and find out who now owns all your debts. You and I know you can't find money to pay off all of that now. I would suggest that when you're well rested you come and have a little chat with me and lets see if we can't come to an amicable agreement. Don't disappoint me or you will be very sorry. See you soon. Ta. (EXITS)

THE CROWD CHEERS AS BUCKINGSWORTH AND HIS TEAM RETREAT.

BLACK-OUT

ACT I, SCENE 9

INSIDE MRS. TERRYLONGE'S HOUSE. WHEN THE LIGHTS COME UP, TREVOR IS AT THE FRONT DOOR.

TREVOR:	(KNOCKING) Hello, hello.
MALIKA:	(FROM INSIDE) Coming, coming. (OPENS DOOR) Hi, can I help you?
TREVOR:	Hello Malika, sorry to disturb you. Is Miss Terrylonge in? I need to speak with her.
MALIKA:	I thought you came to me. (SMILES) Hold on, let me call her. Grandy.
MISS T:	(FROM INSIDE) Malika, are you still at the door? Who are you talking to?
MALIKA:	It's Trevor Grandy.
MISS T:	(ENTERING) Trevor? How you doing? What can I do for you son?
TREVOR:	I want to discuss something serious with you Miss Terrylonge.
MISS T:	What is it my son?
TREVOR:	Well I know you are aware of the problem with the land and thing. Now they want to enter the dance contest. But I honestly don't think that Jonkanoo can win the competition. We all may be evicted.
MISS T:	Don't worry. No one can evict you.
TREVOR:	Well it's not that. We have been trying to raise the money to pay the tax that the government said you are owing. We plan to have a dance in the square.
MISS T:	I think it is a good thing that you young people are doing to save Jonkanoo Village.

TREVOR: Well I just want to get your opinion on it.

TREVOR SHOWS MISS TERRYLONGE THE POSTER ANNOUNCING THE JONKANOO DANCE COMPETITION.

TREVOR: Look at this. They are offering a million dollars to the winner of the National Dance Competition. You can use any authentic Jamaican danceform and Mas Benjy believes that we can do it with Jonkanoo.

MISS T: Well we all know that nobody can beat Jonkanoo Village.

TREVOR: Mas Benjamin has been trying to keep up the Jonkanoo over the years. Well if we enter and win, the prize money of one million dollars can cover the tax.

MISS T: We can invite all di old time dancers to come back and jump.

MALIKA: I will help. (THEY STARE AT HER) Not to dance Jonkanoo, although I am willing to give it a try. But I will work with you to organize it.

TREVOR: We don't have much time to prepare for this contest. First the dance to raise money, then the competition.

MISS T: Let's do it. Let's revive the old Jonkanoo Band and put back the Jonkanoo into the village.

                                                    BLACK-OUT

ACT I, SCENE 10

JONKANOO VILLAGE SQUARE. MALIKA AND TREVOR ARE HEADING A RECRUITMENT DRIVE ON BEHALF OF BENJAMIN FOR THE NEW JONKANOO BAND. THEY ARE MOVING FROM DOOR TO DOOR COLLECTING VOLUNTEERS.

BENJAMIN: If we get enough people to sign up to dance Jonkanoo we can win the competition and win di prize money and pay off the land tax.

TREVOR: I support you Mas Benjamin, but we still need more people.

BENJAMIN: Right, and we don't have plenty time either.

TREVOR: (TO VILLAGERS) So what unno say? You all going to join up? This is our last chance.

MALIKA: Save Jonkanoo Village. Prevent the eviction. Jonkanoo Village needs you now.

TREVOR SEES STAGGER BACK AND GIZZADA IN THE BACKGROUND. THEY APPROACH WITH A SMALL ENTOURAGE.

TREVOR: Stagger Back and Gizzada, why don't you both sign up for the Jonkanoo Band?

MALIKA: Yes, you would make a good Jonkanoo.

GIZZADA: Is who she ah talk? Me look like Jonkanoo? Miss Malika, you bright to come a call me a Jonkanoo.

MALIKA: No Gizzada. What I meant was, with your kind of positive energy and active spirit and tenacity, Jonkanoo Village will do well if you were a part of the dance competition.

GIZZADA: Of course I will. No dance contest can tek place inna Jonkanoo Village and Lady Gizzada no inna it. A wha do her Stagger Back?

STAGGER:	Introducing Lady Gizzada, Jonkanoo Village representative for the National Dance Contest.
GIZZADA:	One thing though, me nah dance di fool-fool Jonkanoo. Strictly dance hall run tings inna dis yah place.
MALIKA:	Well we were thinking of the Jonkanoo.
GIZZADA:	And who is we? And why you hitch on to Trevor like a shadow?
TREVOR:	Yes, we are entering Mas Benjamin Jonkanoo Band in the competition and we hope to win the million dollars.
STAGGER:	Win? How we fi win wid Jonkanoo? Dat a crime scene my yute.
TREVOR:	Mas Benjamin thinks that if we revive the Jonkanoo Band it will give us the best chance to win the competition and the one million dollars.
STAGGER:	And dat is fi unno opinion. Well I say dat is dancehall going take di prize dis time.
GIZZADA:	Well we a go enter another group inna di competition. LAUGHS. Against dis yah posse, unno no stand a chance wid unno idiot Jonkanoo. Jonkanoo ah old time something, Jonkanoo ah foolishness.
MALIKA:	You can't say that. Jonkanoo is our culture.
GIZZADA:	What you know bout culture Miss Malika? How you fi stay a farrin and know what is fi wi culture?
MALIKA:	Well I have studied plenty and I read a lot about these things.
GIZZADA:	Dis yah culture no reach book a farrin yet so yuh couldn't read it.

STAGGER:	Dancehall culture is fi we culture.
GIZZADA:	And me a di queen fi down here. I am following the footsteps of Carlene, Stacey and Junku. Oh so badly.
STAGGER:	Come inna dis my dancers. Dancehall time inna Jonkanoo village. Unno try test this. Plug it eeen.

STAGGER BACK BECKONS TO HIS POSSE. THEY ALL FOLLOW BEHIND LADY GIZZADA MOUTHING DANCEHALL RYTHYMS AND DANCING.

BLACK-OUT

ACT I, SCENE 11

A PRIVATE STUDY INSIDE THE HOUSE OF MR. BUCKINGSWORTH.
MR. B AND MISS T ARE IN A PRIVATE MEETING WHILE ADASA SPIES
ON THE CONVERSATION.

MR. B:	So good of you to come Mrs. Terrylonge. What a pleasure.
MISS T:	The pleasure is all yours I assure you.
MR. B:	Don't be like that. I have your best interest at heart.
MISS T:	Buck-buck Buckingsworth, cut to the chase and don't take me for a fool.
MR. B:	Stop it. Nobody calls me that anymore.
MISS T:	I checked with my creditors and discovered that you have bought up all my debts. And I know you have no good intentions so I should be calling you worst things than that. So what do you want?
MR. B:	Let's make a deal. So Deal or No Deal
MISS T:	I think you better say what's on your mind
MR. B:	I am going to say it fast. (HE ROLLS OPEN THE DEVELOPMENT PLAN FOR THE HOTEL) So tell me how you feel bout this. Deal or no deal?
MISS T:	I don't make deals with the devil. I will pay you the money that is owed. (SHE MOVES TO EXIT)
MR. B:	Stop! Wait. I'm not finished talking with you. Stay right there and let me tell you how this is going to go. I want my money now, cash on the barrel. Now.
MISS T:	You know I can't give it to you right away.

MR. B: Exactly. So now do we understand each other? Hmmm. I will allow you to keep your little ramshackle house on the hill but those squatters on the beach must be evicted now. They already got notice so get them off.

MISS T: I can't do that.

MR. B: You can and you will, or I will close on the loans and you will have nothing. Nothing to live on. Nothing to leave your granddaughter. Nowhere to live. You will become a squatter just like them and I assure you, I don't entertain squatters on MY property. However... If you should agree to my deal I will pay off your property taxes, give you ten percent in the hotel we build on the beach. We will relocate the people on to Cow Island and save your name from disgrace. Now do we have a deal...? I can't hear you....deal or no deal... hmmm? (SHE EXITS) That's what I thought. (ADASA MOVES AWAY)

                                          BLACK-OUT

ACT I, SCENE 12

JONKANOO VILLAGE SQUARE. THE VILLAGERS ARE BUSY PREPARING THE FOR THE BIG DANCE. SOUND SYSTEM, POTS, DRUMS AND STOVES ARE BROUGHT ONTO THE STAGE. SOME DECORATIONS ARE STRUNG UP TO GIVE THE PLACE A FESTIVE MOOD. A BANNER READS "JONKANOO VILLAGE BASHMENT". GIZZADA IS RUNNING THE BAR WHILE STAGGER BACK CONTROLS THE GATE. THE GUESTS COME IN SLOWLY.

GIZZADA: Come on everybody; buy out di bar, full up di place. We haffi mek di money tonight. How much money we collect Stagger Back? We make it yet?

STAGGER: No sah, look like all ah di people dem in here beat di gate.

GIZZADA: Nutten nah gwaan over the bar either. Di drinks nah sell at all. Some ah dem bring dem own drinks inna di place. Dem mean and cheap.

GIZZADA MOVES OVER TO THE SOUND SYSTEM AND TAKES AWAY THE MICROPHONE AND PLEADS WITH THE PEOPLE.

GIZZADA: (TAPS MIKE) Hi, hello, party people. Di bar nah sell. Unno hear me? No more music nah play in here till unno buy out di bar.

TREVOR: How much we make so far Stagger Back?

STAGGER: Is bout one hundred people in here yuh know Mr. Trevor, and no money no collect yet.

TREVOR: You check off the bar and food yet?

STAGGER: Yes. Between Gizzada and the food area we mek three thousand, eight hundred and fifty dollars. We short.

TREVOR: We short by whole heap.

GIZZADA:	Mek me see. (CALCULATES) One million dollars minus three thousand, eight hundred and fifty dollars, dats equal to...hmmm... nine hundred and ninety six thousand, one hundred and fifty dollars and no cents. We short bad.
STAGGER:	Well might as well we just gwaan enjoy we self.

MUSIC UP AND THE FESTIVITIES GO ON. THE MUSIC STOPS ABRUPTLY AND THE LIGHTS COME UP. BUCKINGSWORTH, CORPORAL CLAPPERS AND SHADOW ENTER.

CLAPPERS:	Lock off di dance.
GIZZADA:	Who say so? Which idiot say dat?
CLAPPERS:	Shadow, lock off di music and shet down dance and go a unno yard.
CROWD:	What? Yuh can't do dat.
SHADOW:	No more dance nah keep yasso tonight.
PRECIOUS:	And who give you authority to come down here and lock off fi wi dance?
CLAPPERS:	Permission from the Commissioner of Police. Unno a mek disturbances inna people ears.
SHADOW:	The decent residents of Quadrille Heights are complaining dat dem can't sleep in peace.
PRECIOUS:	Who up dere is complaining?
JOYCE:	Who up there is decent?
MR. B:	I am. As a lawful taxpayer, I demand some peace and tranquility in my home, what I pat for.
MRS. D:	I will not be driven out by a village of parasites and vulgar squatters.
GIZZADA:	Mek me tell yuh something sar..............
CROWD:	Hold her. Hold Gizzada. Hold her back.

AT THIS POINT THERE APPEARS IN THE DISTANCE, A GAUDILY DRESSED EFFIGY OF A WOMAN WEARING A BROAD RIMMED STRAW HAT. SHE APPEARS TALLER THAN THE TREES. SHE MOVES SLOWLY AGAINST THE FENCE.

MRS. D:	Who is that?
MR. B:	What? Is it some kind of joke you all playing on me down here?
MRS. B:	What is this?
PRECIOUS:	Make me talk to her and see what she want.
DONALDS:	Hello Miss lady, who you is mam? Can we help you?

THE MEN GRAB THEIR WEAPONS WHILE THE WOMEN CLUSTER TO THE THE SIDE.

CROWD:	Jeezam peas. Is she. Is she. Dat is Madda Lundi.
VILLAGER:	Duppy Jonkanoo? Mi tell unno say dat dere sinting is a duppy long time.
PRECIOUS:	But dat is not the spirit I did see. And it don't feel the same way at all.
BENJAMIN:	If is Madda Lundi, she don't mean no harm. She come to protect we.
M LUNDI:	Get out!!! All of you get out of Jonkanoo village and leave me in peace.
JOYCE:	No sah. Da duppy yah a tek tings serious.
MRS. D:	I don't find this funny.
DONALDS:	Clappers shoot it. (CLAPPERS IS EQUALLY SCARED)
CLAPPERS:	What sar? Yes sar.
MR. B:	Shoot what? Don't you see she has the right idea? They need to get out.

M LUNDI:	Get out!!! All of you get out of Jonkanoo village and leave me in peace.
MR. B:	Even your own spirits are speaking out about this. You all need to leave. Please do so with dignity. Nobody and nothing wants you here. All you squatters need to leave.

MADDA LUNDI RETREATS AND DISAPPEARS IN THE NIGHT.

VILLAGERS:	Is true him a talk enuh. Nothing nuh right again. Everything gone bad. Jonkanoo Village gone to di dogs. Not even Mada Lundi want us here. Is time to pack up and go.
PRECIOUS:	Don't listen to him. Its some sort of trick. Don't listen to him.
CROWD:	You lucky Precious. Me not staying here inna dis no more. Pure crosses deh pon di land.
M LUNDI:	Leave. I say leave.

CURTAIN

ACT TWO

ACT II, SCENE 1

MAS BENJAMIN'S JONKANOO WORKSHOP. SOME VILLAGERS ARE
ASSISTING WITH THE MAKING OF COSTUMES FOR THE JONKANOO
PARADE. THERE ARE MASKS, HORSE-HEADS, PITCH FORKS AND
OTHER LARGER ITEMS AROUND.

PRECIOUS: Jonkanoo masquerade making time now. We
have to work together so we can ready for
the competition because one finger cyaan
ketch lice. After we done dem here costumes,
then we going do the best Jonkanoo dance
in di parish.

BENJAMIN: We have to get at least ten costumes finished
if we want to jump Jonkanoo this year. Is
good that Miss Terrylonge send some of her
long time frock dem to help make costume.

VILLAGERS: (SING)

What a masquerade in town dis holiday

When we put on Jonkanoo and play

Ribbons and bows and painted faces laugh

Jonkanoo costumes, brightly coloured masks

We painting, we cutting and sewing

We making pretty Jonkanoo masquerade

We laughing, we dancing and we prancing

We dressing-up for the Jonkanoo parade

Listen to the tune of fife and beat of drum

Conch shell and cow horn sounds of fun

Beat the kente drum and scrape the greater

Sounds of Jonkanoo band and much laughter

Bucking, jigging, jumping and wheeling

Head-rolling, foot-pointing and balancing

We dance Jonkanoo from early morning

Jonkanoo masquerade all day till evening

ADASA: I am going to use this costume to play Bellywoman.

PRECIOUS: I soon finish this Pitchy Patchy costume. Me just need some more scrapses. Joyce, make yourself useful. Pass dat bag of scrapses cloth for me. How it look so far?

ZACKY: It looks pretty for true.

BENJAMIN: Precious, as soon as you finish dat one, you can start working on the Police Man.

PRECIOUS: Miss Adasa is adjusting the frock for Bellywoman. When she finish with the machine me will work pon it.

MISS T AND MALIKA ENTER.

PRECIOUS:	Good evening Miss T and Miss Malika. It is so good to see oonoo.
MISS T:	We just come to see how the preparations are coming along.
JOYCE:	Maybe that is what you come to see but me sure Miss Malika come to see something else.
PRECIOUS:	Joyce mind yuh manners.
JOYCE:	I'm just saying. But is a much better look dan di crosses gyal up a Quadrille Heights. (TO MALIKA) Young lady, you see something you like down here in Jamaica? Wat a ting.
TREVOR:	Miss Joyce. Nuh bother embarrass the young lady.
JOYCE:	But what is not dis? Di young lady?
TREVOR:	Miss Joyce! Just stop it alright. Nuh bother wid it right now.
JOYCE:	Ok boss man. I hear yuh.
PRECIOUS:	So Miss T, how does it feel to be back in all of this confusion?
MISS T:	This is home my dear and always will be through good and bad times.
ADASA:	Home? I hope that when the mouth speaks, the ears hear. Glory.
PRECIOUS:	Adasa? Is what happen?
ADASA:	Nothing.
MISS T:	My husband would turn in his grave to see what Buckingsworth is trying to do to you all.
ADASA:	I hope that when he turns in the grave he rolls over and whispers in your ears. Glory.
PRECIOUS:	No man. Adasa, you getting off yuh rockers?

MISS T:	Whatever do you mean Adasa?
ADASA:	Remember I work up at that house enuh ma'am. And I know all the goings on. I see when you made the deal with Buckingsworth to get us off the property. So don't you come here and play hypocrite now.
BENJAMIN:	Adasa.
ADASA:	Its true. Speak the word of truth.
PRECIOUS:	What she talking bout Miss T?
MISS T:	Well, that's not exactly true.
PRECIOUS:	Not exactly…true?
ADASA:	Glory. The lord see-eth into the secret places.
PRECIOUS:	Adasa stop it.
MISS T:	Listen to me. He tried to make a deal with me.
MALIKA:	Grandy?
MISS T:	I had to go and listen to what he said. It turns out I owe him a lot of money now. He bought up all my debts.
TREVOR:	So what we going to do bout it?
JOYCE:	See it deh? She sell we out. I know it woulda happen. See it deh…
TREVOR:	Miss Joyce. Stop it. Let's give her a chance. Everybody stop talk and listen. Miss T, me and you come to an agreement.
MISS T:	Yes we did and that hasn't changed. Is just that in addition to the million dollars for the property tax, I have to find another way to get money to pay off my debts.
BENJAMIN:	So what we going to do now?

TREVOR:	Maybe we can appeal to Mr. Buckingsworth's sense of decency.
MISS T:	He doesn't have any.
ADASA:	But Mrs. Buckingsworth has nuff. She is a decent lady.
MISS T:	That is true. We were very good friends at school before she got married to the devil.
ADASA:	She's still a decent lady ma'am.
TREVOR:	Well maybe we can go talk to her.
PRECIOUS:	No sah, dem would see us coming and call police.
TREVOR:	But Adasa you work there. So maybe you could talk to her and tell her Miss T wants to meet with her in private. And then Miss T. maybe you could convince her to talk to her husband.
ADASA:	I will talk to her Trevor. But I can't promise a ting. That devil man up there is not an easy man. But mek we see what gwaan. If the lord be for us...glory. (SHE EXITS. THERE IS AN UNCOMFORTABLE SILENCE WITH PEOPLE NOT KNOWING WHAT TO SAY)
MISS T:	The house looks pretty. It soon finish? It look like it want another coat of paint.
ZACKY:	Yes Mas Benjamin. It's pretty for true. Dis is the prettiest me ever see Ku-Ku Jonkanoo look since me deh inna this band.
MALIKA:	Ku-Ku Jonkanoo? What is that?
BENJAMIN:	Ku-Ku is the same as Actor Boy. He is going to carry that house on his head. So he has to be strong.
MALIKA:	So who are the other costumes for?

BENJAMIN:	For this year, apart from the usual Devil, Horse-head, Policeman, Bellywoman and Pitchy Patchy, we want to add Jack-in-the-Green.
MALIKA:	Where I am from we know about Jack in the box.
BENJAMIN:	No, not that kind of Jack. Jack-in-the-Green is just smaddy cover up with plenty bush. He look like he is hiding in the bushes.
MALIKA:	Mas Benjamin, why is that horse-head looking at me like that? It looks like a real.
MISS T:	Dat is the real ting mi dear. Dis is the real jawbone of a horse what dead over thirty years now. See it here.
MALIKA:	Grandy, that dead horse-head looks like a horse duppy for real.
BENJAMIN:	You learning though. Is who telling you bout duppies and such things?
MISS T:	Remember is my grand daughter enuh Mas Benjy. I not going to let her grow with me and don't know her Jamaican roots and culture. But on another note, what is this I'm hearing about duppy coming to the square?
BENJAMIN:	That is some trickery. I don't believe that was no Madda Lundy. Somebody up to no good and I suspect we all know who it is.
JOCYCE:	Trickery or not, me never see people run so fast in my life. And some a dem still running.
BENJAMIN:	When I look round di square I never notice you either Miss Joyce. I barely see the back of your head disappear down di road.
JOYCE:	You don't worry bout dat. Anyway, me tired now yuh hear sar. Me a go a me yard.
PRECIOUS:	But yuh no lift yuh hand from yuh come Joyce?

JOYCE:

Oh my Miss Precious. Yuh never take yuh eye and see when Miss Adasa ask me to pass her the needle and thread and me walk all the way over deh so and stretch give it to her over yasso. Me work ma'am.

PRECIOUS:

All right Miss Joyce. Tomorrow, I will make sure you do plenty work. You can help me cut bush and mek di Jack-in-the-Green costume. Miss T, all of we ready. We all on the same side ma'am. Mas Benjamin, see yuh in the morning.

BLACK-OUT

ACT II, SCENE 2

OUTSIDE BUCKINGSWORTH'S HOUSE. ASP CLAPPERS HAS A MEETING WITH BUCKINGSWSORTH TO MAKE HIS REPORT.

CLAPPERS:	(WHISPERS) Mr. B, which part yuh deh? Me see dem sar.
MR. B:	What are they planning? What are they locked up in that place doing Clappers?
CLAPPERS:	Dem ah make Jonkanoo costume sar. Plenty costume.
MR. B:	Costumes for what?
CLAPPERS:	Dem ah get ready fi enter di dance competition too sar.
MR. B:	Enter what? These people are brighter than the Negril lighthouse. Before they start packing up their belongings and clear off my land. How do they find time to enter a dance competition?
CLAPPERS:	Nobody nah pack nutten sar. No sar, it no look like dem a leave sar. Dem nah go nowhere Missa B.
MR. B:	There must be something I can do to get them off.
CLAPPERS:	Lock dem up sar. Arrest dem fi trespassing pon yuh property. Di law will back you.
MR. B:	I don't have to lock dem up. No way they can come up with that breed of money to pay the taxes, so they will be off the land whether they like it or not. (HE EXITS)
SHADOW:	Ahm. Mr Clappers sar.
CLAPPERS:	Yes Shadow.

154

SHADOW:	You don't have any second thoughts bout this whole thing sar?
CLAPPERS:	What you mean?
SHADOW:	Well the truth sar is that I was thinking...
CLAPPERS:	You?
SHADOW:	Yes sar. And it occurred to me that maybe Mr. Buckingsworth not in the right enuh sar.
CLAPPERS:	What?
SHADOW:	Yes sar is just that. Me and you grow up with these people sar. So how all of a sudden, now that we have likkle authority, dem have to be in the wrong and Mr. Buckingsworth in the right sar? And me just thinking that it don't feel right.
CLAPPERS:	Shut up. Shut up. You just shut up yuh mouth right now and just listen to me. Thinking is not for everybody, you understand me. Mr. Buckingsworth dem is decent people.
SHADOW:	But Miss Precious, Miss T and Mas Benjamin dem decent too sar.
CLAPPERS:	Shut up.
SHADOW:	And me grow up with Trevor and Stagger Back.
CLAPPERS:	Not another word. I won't report yuh for this or demote you cause I know you just don't know better. You can't tell decent people when you see dem cause you don't have no class. I have been associating with these people for much longer than you and so I knows dese tings. Don't let me hear you with it again. HE EXITS.

BLACK-OUT

ACT II, SCENE 3

INSIDE MAS BENJAMIN'S JONKANOO WORKSHOP. THE LAST SET OF VILLAGERS BID GOOD NIGHT TO MAS BENJAMIN. THEY LEAVE THE WORKSHOP AND MAS BENJAMIN STARTS CLERING UP THE WORKSHOP AND CHECKING OFF THE WORK ACCOMPLISHED. HE NOTICES SOME MOVEMENT OF THE HORSE-HEAD BUT PASSES IT OFF.

BENJAMIN: Aye sah. Me think me see the horse-head light up inna the dark. Me eyes playing tricks.

AS MAS BENJAMIN TURNS OFF THE LIGHTS AND PREPARES TO LOCK UP THE WORKSHOP. THE THREE JONKANOO CHARACTERS AND A LARGE WOMAN DANCE AROUND HIM BUT HE CAN'T HEAR IT. IT IS THE SAME ENORMOUS WOMAN SEEN EARLIER BY THE RESIDENTS AT THE DANCE. MAS BENAJMIN STANDS AND FACES MADDA LUNDI. THEY SEEM TO BE COMMUNICATING.

BLACK-OUT

ACT II, SCENE 4

INSIDE THE HOUSE OF THE BUCKINGHAM'S

MRS. B:	Sarah. Sarah. Wherever is that girl. Sarah.
SARAH:	(YAWNING) Yes mommy.
MRS. B:	I feel I haven't seen you in ages. What's the matter with you? And why are you so tired.
SARAH:	Ahhm… nothing mommy…nothing…
MRS. B:	Sarah Begonia Rothschild Buckingsworth. Don't lie to me.
SARAH:	I can't do it mummy. I can't…
MR. B:	(ENTERS) What the devil is going on here?
SARAH:	I didn't tell her anything daddy.
MR. B:	What are you saying Sarah?
MRS. B:	Yes. What are you saying Sarah?
SARAH:	Nothing.
MRS. B:	Don't lie to me.
MR. B:	It's nothing.
MRS. B:	How you know that? (SHE GOES TO SARAH AND HOLDS HER) What are you not telling me?
SARAH:	(SHE RATTLES) I was just helping out daddy, with the Madda Lundi thing because he said he needed me to play a little game with the local villagers. So I used some of my old Halloween costumes and scared the people with an effigy. I am sorry daddy…sorry mommy. (SHE BREAKS DOWN)
MRS. B and MR. B:	Sarah!!!
MRS. B:	Nosworth.

MR. B: Yes dear? Look, I can't talk right now. I'm very busy.

MRS. B: Stop. I can't believe you. Why would you do such a thing to our daughter?

MR. B: Look don't get all high and mighty with me Miss trust fund baby. You have nothing in common with those local commoners down there. So what if I'm playing a little prank on them.

MRS. B: With our daughter? I can't find the words.

MRS. B: That's good dear, because I have to go. (HE EXITS)

ADASA: (ENTERS) Mrs. B, can I talk to you a minute ma'am?

MRS. B: Not right now Adasa, I'm sorry I just have too much to...

ADASA: Is really urgent and important ma'am. Please.

MRS. B: Ok. Adasa. (THEY SIT)

BLACK-OUT

ACT II, SCENE 5

PATHWAY OUTDOOR. TREVOR WALKS MALIKA HOME FROM THE
COSTUME WORKSHOP.

MALIKA:	It was kind of you to walk me home Trevor.
TREVOR:	I wouldn't let you alone come all the way up here in the dark Malika.
MALIKA:	Thanks. Grandy must be waiting up on me. See you tomorrow.
TREVOR:	So you ready to go inside already? Spend some time and enjoy the night. I am sure you not accustomed to seeing clear skies and stars like this abroad where you live.
MALIKA:	Well that's true. But…
TREVOR:	Don't say but. Just sit on the verandah and enjoy the night. Ahmm.. Malika….
MAILKA:	Yes Trevor.
TREVOR:	Ahmm…
MALIKA:	Is what you afraid to say it?
TREVOR:	Afraid? To say what?
MALIKA:	Whatever is on your mind.
TREVOR:	No. You afraid?
MALIKA:	Afraid of what?
TREVOR:	Madda Lundi? (HE MIMMICS MADDA LUNDI) I am Madda Lundi.
MALIKA:	That's not funny Trevor. You frightened me.
TREVOR:	Sorry Malika, I didn't mean to scare you like that. I was joking. There must be some explanation to all those fables. I don't believe anything like that.

159

MALIKA: There is so much to learn about this village.

TREVOR: Why don't you stay and learn it, I will teach you.

                                              BLACK-OUT

ACT II, SCENE 6

THE VILLAGERS ARE GATHERED OUTSIDE MISS TERRYLONGE'S HOUSE. THEY ARE THERE TO LEARN TO DO THE JONKANOO AND TO PRACTICE THE ENTRY TO THE JONKANOO JAMBOREE NATIONAL COMPETITION.

PRECIOUS: Order, order. Welcome, welcome. We are few but we are thankful. I am glad that unno could come to the practice.

MALIKA: We are expecting about twenty-five people Miss Precious. Many more than this signed up. I am sure they are coming.

PRECIOUS: Well I just want to thank Miss Terrylonge for letting us use her yard for the practice.

MAS BENJAMIN ENTERS WITH SOME COSTUMES IN HIS HAND.

BENJAMIN: Right, unno ready to try on the costume. Remember what character yuh playing and just take the matching costume. More are coming, but these are just for the practice this evening. Unno ready to learn the Jonkanoo dance? Dancing time.

THE VILLAGERS LEARN THE BASIC JONKANOO STEPS FROM MAS BENJAMIN AS THE LIGHTS FADE.

LIGHTS FADE

ACT II, SCENE 7

LIGHTS CROSS FADE TO THE BUCKINGSWORTH HOUSE IN QUADRILLE HEIGHTS. MRS. DONALDS IS TEACHING MR. DONALDS, SARAH AND THE BUCKINGSWORTHS THEIR QUADRILLE DANCE

MRS. D: Heads up and back upright. When you do the Quadrille you must be stately like royalty. Remember this is Ballroom style dance and not Jonkanoo. So after me, one, two, three. And move, and smile, take your partner and gentleman bow and ladies curtsy elegantly. (THEY DANCE) One more time.

                                                    LIGHTS FADE

ACT II, SCENE 8

LIGHTS CROSS FADE AND THE ACTION RETURNS TO JONKANOO VILLAGE. ADASA ENTERS IN THE MIDDLE OF THE JONKANOO PRACTICE SESSION. SHE IS DRESSED IN FULL WHITE WITH HER HEAD WRAPPED.

JOYCE: A which part you a go dress so Sister Adasa? Dis is not church.

ADASA: Get thee behind me Satan. I am always with the Lord my sister and the church is always with me.

BENJAMIN: All right now. Time now fi learn di basics of Jonkanoo. Put unno foot out. Jump pon one foot so. Then jump pon yuh other back so. Then spin so. No. Jump pon yuh back foot and jump pon yuh front foot.

JOYCE: Which one a mi foot a front and which one a back sar?

BENJAMIN: All right me going make you wear di Cow head so all yuh have to do is bend down and buck. Yuh can buck?

JOYCE: Yes sar. Like this? (DEMONSTRATES)

BENJAMIN: Good. Now back to the rest of unno. Try the dance one more time.

JOYCE: Put some more rhythm inna di music and it will sound better.

MUSICIANS GIVE IT AN UPBEAT AND THE GROUP TRIES THE DANCE AGAIN. THERE IS AN ENERGETIC PRESENTATION OF A JONKANOO DANCE WHICH IS BROKEN UP BY STAGGER BACK AND GIZZADA ALONG ACCOMPANIED BY A DANCEHALL POSSE. THEY ENTER AND CIRCLE THE REHEARSAL.

STAGGER:	A what dat? Unno really tink say dem dere old time dance can win inna dem yah modern time?
BENJAMIN:	Dis is Jonkanoo Village and we will jump Jonkanoo till we die.
GIZZADA:	Well since we no dead yet, we ah go enter another dance fi represent Jonkanoo Village at the dance contest. Dancehall style.
STAGGER:	Change di rhthym Me. Selector. Give me more bass. Come in my massive. Mek we show dem how it go. If yuh ready fi dance say Whoooiii.

STAGGER BACK TAKES THE MICROPHONE AND LEADS HIS DANCERS THROUGH A SHORT DANCEHALL ROUTINE.

STAGGER:	(SINGS)

Do di dancehall Jonkanoo

Dance di dancehall Jonkanoo

Now, make me show you what to do

Follow me now, and dance di Jonkanoo

Hop pon one foot and den pon di other foot

Back foot, right foot then spin pon one foot

Cowhead bend down low and buck

Devil tek yuh fork and do di jook

Gallop and kick yuh foot horse-head

Shake pitchy patchy, shake up yuh head

Hop pon one foot and den pon di other foot

Back foot, right foot then spin pon one foot

BENJAMIN:	Dancehall Jonkanoo? Rubbish.

STAGGER: We are going to take it to a higher lever. Yuh
                     get di drift? Higher level? (LAUGHS)

MAS BENJAMIN INSTRUCTS HIS BAND AND DANCERS AND
THEY BEGIN THEIR ROUTINE AGAIN. THE DANCEHALL DANCERS
CHALLENGE. THERE IS A DANCE-OFF (CLASH) BETWEEN THE
DANCEHALL DANCERS AND THE JONKANOO DANCERS AS THF
LIGHTS FADE.

                                                  BLACK-OUT

ACT II, SCENE 9

JONKANOO BEACH VILLAGE SQUARE. MISS T MEETS UP WITH THE VILLAGERS.

MISS T:	(ENTERING) What is this I am hearing? I heard that we are entering two dances from Jonkanoo Village for the dance competition.
PRECIOUS:	Well to tell you di trutth mam, its Gizzada and the Stagger Back. Dem say dem entering another dance.
MISS T:	Well what that means now is that we have two chances of winning. May the better Jonkanoo dance win the prize.
MALIKA:	They're not doing a Jonkanoo dance grandma, they doing dancehall.
MISS T:	Dancehall from Jonkanoo Village? Don't make me laugh today.
PRECIOUS:	It's the truth she is telling mam. Dancehall dem ah do.
MISS T:	I hope they don't embarrass themselves on the national television. So what is Quadrille Heights entering?
PRECIOUS:	I get to understand that Mr. Buckingsworth paid smaddy dem call choreographer to come in from Kingston to teach them a Quadrille Ballroom dance.
MISS T:	Jonkanoo Village has enough dancers? Who is dancing Pitchy Patchy?
PRECIOUS:	We might no bother wid Pitchy Patchy Miss T, because nobody no catch dat riddim yet.

MISS T: No. You can't jump Jonkanoo without Pitchy Patchy. Pitchy Patchy is the life of the Jonkanoo band. Without Pitchy Patchy there is no Jonkanoo.

MALIKA: Let Trevor do it Grandy. He has the perfect rhythm.

PRECIOUS: Trevor can drop foot, but I am not sure if he is interested. He is busy organizing things.

MALIKA: I will ask him. He will do it for me. Trust me.

MISS T: Send to call him. I will teach him all I know bout Pitchy Patchy tonight. We still have time. Trevor will learn Pitchy Patchy.

BLACK-OUT

ACT II, SCENE 10

TREVOR MEETS UP WITH SARAH SECRETLY ON THE BEACH LATE EVENING.

TREVOR:	What is it Sarah? I got your message that you needed to see me urgently. I can't stay long because Miss T is going to teach me Pitchy Patchy tonight so I can lead our dance for the competition.
SARAH:	I hear that she has some secret Pitchy Patchy moves to teach you.
TREVOR:	And you know that we will win the competition. Anyway, what is it you need to see me about?
SARAH:	My daddy has some better news for you; he asked me to deliver it to you personally.
TREVOR:	I am the last person your father would want you to be with now. What is it?
SARAH:	You don't have to dance, you can get a good job and earn lots of money.
TREVOR:	What yuh mean?
SARAH:	He has a job for you. It pays a lot of money. But he wants you to come tonight to sign the contract and begin working right away.
TREVOR:	Not right now. I have to go learn the Pitchy Patchy dance.
SARAH:	Pitchy Patchy rubbish. You can't turn down a good job offer with my father just for a stupid Jonkanoo dance.
TREVOR:	It is not rubbish and it is not stupid. If we win that money, we could save Jonaknoo Village.

CLAPPERS AND SHADOW ENTER FROM BEHIND THROW A SACK OVER TREVOR'S HEAD. TREVOR PUTS UP A FIGHT BUT SHADOW AND CLAPPERS OVERPOWER HIM. THEY TIE HIM UP AND PULL HIM ASIDE. MR. B ENTERS.

CLAPPERS:	If you can't save your sorry little self, how yuh a go save di whole village?
MR. B:	Pitchy Patchy has fallen. There won't be any Pitchy Patchy in this dance tonight. Let him spend the night out here on the beach wid di mosquitoes until the competition over. (LAUGHS)
SARAH:	What you going to do with him Daddy? Please don't hurt him. I am sorry Trevor.
MR. B:	Take him away. Far away. (HE TAKES SARAH AND EXITS)
SHADOW:	I don't feel good about this Clappers. This is not police work.
CLAPPERS:	ASP Clappers to you.
SHADOW:	You are only ASP to me when you act like police. And dis is not police work...sar.
CLAPPERS:	So what you going to do about it?
SHADOW:	I going to leave you to it sar. I can't do this. In fact, I think I am going to make a report.
CLAPPERS:	Mek which report. You will be just as guilty.
SHADOW:	We will see. (HE EXITS)
CLAPPERS:	Come back. Come here. I say come here. Who dat. Is who dat I hear? (THERE IS A STRANGE SOUND) No man, I know that you are not real. Is Missa Buckingsworth set up di fake duppy fi frighten di people. So don't try to fool me. Who is that? (HE RUNS OFF)

AS CLAPPERS PREPARES TO LIFT TREVOR, MADDA LUNDI APPEARS. THIS TIME SHE IS ACCOMPANIED BY THREE JONKANOO SPIRITS. THEY BLOCK THE PATHWAY. THERE IS A STRUGGLE FOR TREVOR. MADDA LUNDI AND HER SPIRITS TORMENT CLAPPERS, HE RUNS OFF LEAVING TREVOR BEHIND. THE JONKANOO SPIRITS LIFT TREVOR AND TAKE HIM AWAY TO A SECRET CAVE.

BLACK-OUT

ACT II, SCENE 11

SECRET CAVE OF THE JONKANOO SPIRITS – A STRANGELY
DECORATED CAVE ADORNED WITH LARGE JONKANOO MASKS.
THE AIR IS FILLED WITH FIFE AND DRUM. THE SPIRITS ARE LED IN
A RITUAL TO REVIVE TREVOR. THEY DANCE AROUND HIM. BY THE
TIME HE COMES TO HE APPEARS TO BE IN A TRANCE.

TREVOR:	Where am I? Who is dis? Who you?
M LUNDI:	Madda Lundi. My name is Madda Lundi.
TREVOR:	(SLAPS HIMSELF) Trevor, wake up. Wake up man. Madda Lundi? There is no Madda Lundi? Which part me deh? (HE TRIES TO LEAVE BUT IS BLOCKED BY THE JONKANOO SPIRITS) Who are you? You all look like Pitchy Patchy. Somebody playing a trick on me? Where am I? I don't have time for dis. I have to go learn to dance Pitchy Patchy.
M LUNDI:	Dance Pitchy Patchy? You cannot dance Pitchy Patchy if you don't believe in yourself and your culture.
TREVOR:	Is just a dance contest so some people doing dancehall and others doing Jonkanoo.
M LUNDI:	Jonkanoo is the dance of Jonkanoo Village. And no matter how much dancehall you do you must maintain your Jonkanoo culture.
TREVOR:	Jonkanoo is a dying tradition, but I am willing to do it because no one wants to do Pitchy Patchy.
M Lundi:	It cannot die if you all respect it. It is your only hope of remaining on the land. Learn it, understand it and respect it.
TREVOR:	So how I going learn to dance then? Isnt it too late?

M LUNDI: We will teach you. Let us fill your body with our spirits and your bones with our rhythm.

THE SPIRITS ENGAGE TREVOR IN AN ENERGETIC 'PITGHY PATCHY' DANCE ROUTINE. THEY CONTINUE TO DANCE AS THE SCENE CHANGES.

BLACK-OUT

ACT II, SCENE 12

JONKANOO VILLAGE SQUARE. THE SCENE IS SET FOR THE JONKANOO JAMBOREE NATIONAL DANCE COMPETITION. THERE IS MUCH EXCITEMENT IN THE VILLAGE SQUARE AS CONTESTANTS AND ONLOOKERS GET READY FOR THE START OF THE COMPETITION. THE MASTER OF CEREMONIES MOVES TO THE MICROPHONE AND STARTS THE PROGRAMME. LOCAL DIGNITARIES ARE SEATED ON THE PLATFORM.

MC:	Special distinguished guests, ladies and gentlemen, Welcome to the National Dance Competition, held this year in our parish. As we have mentioned before, the winner gets a prize of one million dollars. Yes, one million dollars... This year we have seen numerous entries from various districts...
MISS T:	And not one of them exciting if you ask me. Almost every other group doing dancehall and is the same exact dance if you ask me. No variety. If you put all of the dances together, they look like one long dance. At least when we see the one or two folk dances, you see people getting creative wid wi culture.
MALIKA:	Oh Grandy, I'm so excited. I can't wait to see Jonkanoo Village perform. I'm so glad you took me here to Jamaica to experience all of this.
MISS T:	I had to do that my dear. Marcus Garvey say people who don't know dem history and culture...
MALIKA:	Is like a tree without roots. I know Grandy. I know.

MC:	And now we have another group, the beautiful ballroom dancers of Quadrille Heights district. Please put your hands together and welcome on stage, the beautiful, regal and stately Quadrille Heights dancers.
MISS T:	I teach you well enuh. I am very proud of you.
MALIKA:	Thanks Grandy. Ahm. I'm going to go look for Trevor.
MISS T:	I see that you really take a shine to dat bwoy. Heh.
MALIKA:	Well...ahm... he's really nice, and...
MISS T:	You run along and say hi. But hurry back, I want you to experience all the performances.
MALIKA:	Yes Grandy.

QUADRILLE HEIGHTS DANCERS PERFORM A TRADITIONAL JAMAICAN QUADRILLE DANCE. THE JUDGES AND AUDIENCE LIKE IT AND EXPRESS LOUDLY. MAS BENJAMIN AND PRECIOUS ARE PEEKING FROM THE SIDE WITH SOME OF THE DANCERS FROM THE JONKANOO VILLAGE. THEY COMMENT ON QUADRILLE HEIGHT'S DANCE WHILE THE JUDGES CONFER.

PRECIOUS:	Mas Benajamin yuh see dat? Dem look pretty for true. Dem costumes look like they come from America.
BENJAMIN:	Yes and dem can dance good.
PRECIOUS:	Laad Gad. Dem must win di prize. Wha we aguh do...
BENJAMIN:	Lawks Precious. Don't watch the competition. Unno just go out there and do unno best.
PRECIOUS:	Mi just nervous. Where is Trevor? Anybody see Trevor?

MALIKA ARRIVES NEAR THE JONKANOO VILLAGE DANCERS.

BENJAMIN:	Me nuh see him. No. Me did ah wonder where him gone.
PRECIOUS:	Him have to be here. Malika. Where is Trevor?
MALIKA:	I thought he was with you Miss Precious.
PRECIOUS:	Him not here.

THERE IS A WHISPER IN THE CROWD. TREVOR IS MISSING.

BENJAMIN:	We need him now. Di Jonkanoo can't dance without Pitchy Patchy.
MC:	On with the show. We have only two more entries to go ladies and gentlemen and they are both from Jonkanoo Village. One is a new Dancehall performance and the other is the traditional Jonkanoo called *'Jonkanoo Jamboree'* from Mas Benjamin and his band.
BANJAMIN:	Mr. Emcee. Hold di programme. We can't find Trevor.
MR. B:	(TO BENJAMIN) The show must go on. If a dancer is missing, then they will have to use a substitute, or do without him. (LAUGHS) Where is Pitchy Patchy?
MC:	Ladies and gentlemen, indeed, the show must go on. Please welcome on stage first to represent Jonkanoo Village...
PRECIOUS:	What we an go do?
MISS T:	Stagger Back and Gizzada, unno come here. Stagger Back, you have to dance Pitchy Patchy.
STAGGER:	What mam? Me no come yah fi dance Jonkanoo mam.
MISS T:	Don't argue wid me Stagger Back. Put on the costume and do it.
STAGGER:	I can't do that ma'am...

PRECIOUS: Stagger Back. Shut yuh mouth and let the lady speak. And Gizzada, you draw near too. Cause is time to stop all di foolishness now. We is one Jonkanoo village and we going act like it to save our community. Talk Ms T.

MISS T: I want you all to listen to me. This is more than just a dance competition right now. We are fighting our survival. Yes all a we. I need this as much as you and If is one thing I know about us as a people, is that when trouble tek we, we hold ranks. All a we need to move away from we divisions now and pull together cause this is the only way we aregoing win. So Mas Benjy and Stagger Back I want you to come together and talk it out right now about how you can put the Jonkanoo and the Dancehall together and make one strong entry from Jonkanoo Village. We don't have time. I am going over to stall the Emcee.

MISS TERRYLONGE MOVES TO THE EMCEE AND WHISPERS TO HIM. HE APPEARS CONFUSED BUT RETURNS TO THE PODIUM AND CONTINUES.

MC: Ladies and Gentlemen. There has been a last minute change. Jonkanoo Village will not be represented by two groups today. They have merged to become one. Let us welcome the final group on stage. From Jonkanoo Village it is 'Jonkanoo Jamboree inna Dancehall Style'!

THE MUSIC FOR THIS PERFORMANCE IS A FUSION OF THE JONKANOO RYTHYM CROSSED-OVER WITH DANCEHALL. THE JONKANOO FIFE AND DRUM BAND ACCOMPANIES THE DANCERS. LEADING THE GROUP IS A MODERN DAY PITCHY PATCHY, STAGGER BACK. JONKANOO VILLAGE PRESENTS A JAMBOREE OF A WIDE RANGE OF ELABORATELY DESIGNED COSTUMED JONKANOO CHARACTERISTICS.

MADDA LUNDI EMERGES, TAKES CENTRE STAGE AND LEADS THE REST OF THE DANCERS IN A TRANCE. THE DANCE GETS BIGGER THAN LIFE AS MADDA LUNDI AND HER JONKANOO PITCHY PATCHY SPIRITS ESCORT A MYSTERIOUS LEAD DANCER, "PITCHY PATCHY" ON STAGE. THERE IS A DANCE-OFF BETWEEN THE TWO PITCHY PATCHY DANCERS.

VILLAGERS: Is Madda Lundi dat? Pitchy Patchy? Is who is di other Pitchy Patchy? Who is di real Pitchy Pitchy? Is two Pitchy Patchy.

PITCHY PATCHY LEAVES AND OTHER DANCERS ENTER FROM THE AUDIENCE ON STILTS AND APPEAR FROM THE AIR ON ROPES. THEY DISPLAY AN EXCITING AND COLOURFUL REVELRY. MADDA LUNDI AND HER SPIRITS SLIP AWAY IN THE DARK. THE MYSTERIOUS PITCHY PATCHY REMOVES HIS MASK. IT IS TREVOR. A STARTLED MALIKA RUSHES TO TREVOR AND PULLS HIM ASIDE. THE ACTIVITIES CONTINUE IN BACKGROUND.

MALIKA: Wow Trevor. That was great. Where did you learn to dance like that? Where were you?

TREVOR: It's a long story. Let's say, I was tied up and led by the spirit of Jonkanoo.

MALIKA: And your Pitchy Patchy costume is so colourful and pretty. Who made it? It is so original.

TREVOR: Original indeed. Pretty yes, but nothing to compare to you.

TREVOR AND MALIKA MERGE WITH THE CROWD AGAIN AS THE ACTION SHIFTS BACK TO THE MAIN PERFORMANCE STAGE.

MC: Well, well, well, Ladies and Gentlemen. The judges have made their decision. (HE LOOKS AT THE PAPER) Second place in the National Dance competition is Bamboo Belly District. (CROWD APPLAUDS) And now, for the Champion Dancer. The winner of this year's National Dance Competition is "Jonkanoo Jamboree inna Dancehall Style" from Jonkanoo Village. One Million Dollars.

TREVOR AND STAGGER BACK COLLECT THE HUGE CHEQUE AND TROPHY ON BEHALF OF JONKANOO VILLAGE. THE DANCERS HUG EACH OTHER AND THE IDENTITY BEHIND EACH JONKANOO CHARACTER IS REVEALED WHEN THE MASKS ARE REMOVED.

GIZZADA:	(CHEERING) Money O, One million dollars. Stagger Back, now we have nuff money.
STAGGER:	Nuh say nutten.
PRECIOUS:	We do it. Thank you father God.
BENJAMIN:	Thank you too Madda Lundi.
PRECIOUS:	Now nobody can move we off Jonkanoo Village, Amen.
MISS T:	Thank you God for deliverance. I will sub-divide the property. Now, everybody will have their own legal title for their own little piece of property.
CROWD:	Thank you Miss T. God bless you. We love you. You a Jonkanoo mumma.
MISS T:	I should also be thanking you.
MALIKA:	I think it is so wonderful being here Grandy.
MISS T:	I know you would say that.
MALIKA:	And now that I'm here I don't want to go anywhere else.
MISS T:	I know. You think I don't know that? You have helped to bring back pride to Jonkanoo Village. Enjoy unno self cause Jonkanoo Village is being reborn.

A REPRISAL OF THE JONKANOO PRESENTATION. THE JONKANOO BAND LED BY PITCHY PATCHY STREAMS ACROSS THE STAGE AS THE CURTAIN CLOSES.

VILLAGERS: (SING)
                  Jonkanoo Jamboree again
                  Jonkanoo time again

                  Come celebrate don't be scared my friend
                  Jonkanoo time again
                  Jonkanoo Village is now our own
                  Fife and drum music in our bone
                  We ketch fish and do Jonkanoo dance
                  Nyam fry fish and jump and prance

                  Jonkanoo Jamboree again
                  Jonkanoo time again
                  Come celebrate don't be scared my friend
                  Jonkanoo time again

                  We born and grow inna Jonkanoo
                  We proud to dance the Jonkanoo
                  We stand and fight for Jonkanoo
                  Live we life

                  Jonkanoo Jamboree again
                  Jonkanoo time again
                  Come celebrate don't be scared my friend
                  Jonkanoo time again

                                                CURTAIN